CURRY

CLASSIC AND CONTEMPORARY

VIVEK SINGH

CURRY

CLASSIC AND CONTEMPORARY

ABSOLUTE PRESS **A.**

First published in Great Britain in 2008

This paperback edition first published in 2010 by
Absolute Press
Scarborough House
29 James Street West
Bath BA1 2BT
Phone 44 (0) 1225 316013
Fax 44 (0) 1225 445836
E-mail info@absolutepress.co.uk
Website www.absolutepress.co.uk

Publisher Jon Croft
Commissioning Editor Meg Avent
Editorial Assistant Andrea O'Connor
Designer Matt Inwood
Design Assistant Claire Siggery
Editor Jane Middleton
Photography Cristian Barnett
Food Styling Vivek Singh and Abdul Yaseen
Props Styling Cynthia Inions

ISBN 13: 9781906650407
Printed and bound in Slovenia on behalf
of Latitude Press

A note about the text
This book is set in Sabon and
Trajan. Sabon was designed by
Jan Tschichold in 1964. The roman
design is based on type by Claude
Garamond, whereas the italic
design is based on types by Robert
Granjon. Trajan was designed in
1989 by Carol Twombly, and is
based on classic Roman letterforms.

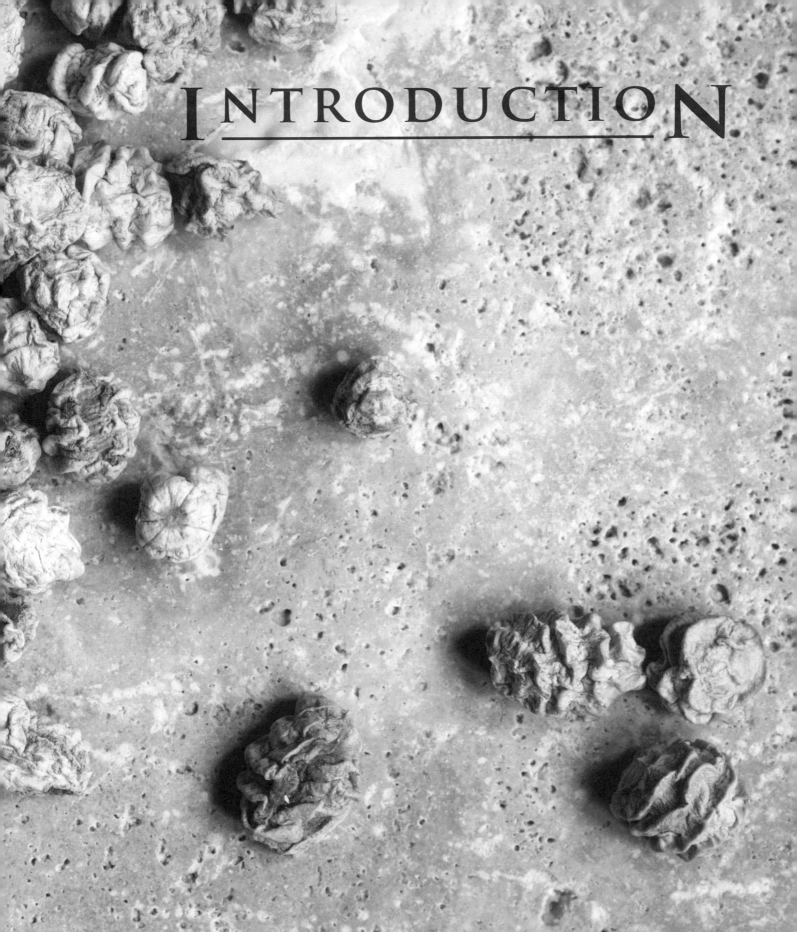

INTRODUCTION

ORIGINS AND MYTHS

Curry is hugely popular throughout the world, yet in India, the place where it all began, the term barely exists. When I finished writing this book, I went through my old Indian menus to make sure I hadn't missed anything out and hardly came across the word at all. I was so surprised – and so concerned to find an authentic definition – that I decided to ask people in India itself, what they understood by curry.

My first port of call was the busy metropolis of Mumbai. Everyone there was very well informed about the latest culinary trends in London and New York, yet when I asked them to define curry there was a palpable hesitation. I looked at menus all over the city and came across just one reference to it. So I headed inland to see if I could find out more there. Bilaspur is a small town at the heart of central India, where most families cook 18 meals a week at home on average. There, too, people struggled to come up with a definition of curry for me; some confused it with kadhai, the Indian wok, while most dismissed the question as absurd, arguing, quite reasonably, that you couldn't possibly group such a large variety of wonderful dishes under a single umbrella. My mother came up with three possible answers: one a soup-style dish made with

yoghurt (kadhi); another a style of cooking (kadhai-style) and third a cooking utensil (kadhai again).

Contrast this with the West, and particularly the UK, where the word curry has come to stand for an entire genre of cooking from Southeast Asia. While it mostly refers to meat, seafood or vegetarian dishes, braised with spices in a sauce, it can also describe spicy stir-fries and dry dishes.

One school of thought links curry to the Tamil word *kari*, or *karee*, meaning sauce. A more plausible explanation, however, is that when British officers in the East India Company were stationed in Chennai (known then as Madras), they would ask the local staff what was being cooked and were told 'curry', or, a mixture. Even though the dishes were quite different every day, the description remained the same – curry. This saved the effort of trying to translate and explain individual dishes, and would account for the British understanding of curry as a complete genre. It is possible that what started as an oversimplification was responsible for one of the biggest misunderstandings in culinary history. It seems that there is no such thing as an authentic definition of curry after all.

THE INDIAN ART OF SPICING

I have come to accept that everyone has their own personal expectations of a curry, whether it's a dish in a standard British curry house or a blanket term for the cooking of an entire subcontinent. Although authenticity might be an illusion, however, what is vital is the role that spices have to play.

When I was cooking at the Aberdeen Marina Club in Hong Kong many years ago, I was rather offended to be told that the guests expected the food to be hotter. In revenge, I kept increasing the amount of chillies in each dish until they started begging for milder food! The things one does as a young man...it did not occur to me then that this would have been an ideal opportunity to introduce those guests to sophisticated, balanced and well-rounded Indian cooking, rather than just playing up to their prejudices. Indian food is about far more than chilli heat. There is a huge repertoire of spices to explore, not just for their heat but for other qualities too: coriander for cooling, cloves for flavour and heat of a different kind, saffron for fragrance, mace and cardamom for their aroma. It is the combination of spices that makes each curry unique.

The art of spicing in India is arguably the most sophisticated and complex in the world. In other cuisines, spices tend to be used in isolation or in simple combinations. Indian cooking relies on an intimate knowledge of the way spices work together – not just their flavours but also their textures, the sequence in which they are added to a dish, and how long they are cooked. It is an exciting and challenging way of cooking, and one in which there is always something new to learn. This brings me on to the subject of ready-made curry powders. The very idea of an all-purpose seasoning blend that can be added to any curry is simply outrageous. Most dishes don't need all the spices they contain anyway, and it is always best to grind

what you need when you need it rather than buying ready-ground spices, which lose much of their flavour, appearance and aroma within two weeks.

Historically, spices were used in India for a variety of reasons. Foremost among these, of course, was flavour, but they were just as important for preservation. In the days before refrigeration, spices helped to prolong the shelf life of fresh ingredients, and were also used to tenderise meat. Traditional Ayurvedic medicine relies on spices for certain health benefits. Besides using spices to treat various ailments, an Ayurvedic practitioner will assess a person's body type and advise which spices and other foods are beneficial for them to consume and which best avoided. It is common knowledge in India that cumin aids digestion, while coriander is an antipyretic which has a cooling effect on the body and is often used to reduce fever in children. Fennel seeds also aid digestion and are used as a mouth freshener. Turmeric is an effective antiseptic and is frequently used to treat minor cuts, burns and wounds.

Although Indian spicing can be highly complex, the cooking techniques for curry are generally very simple. One of the most common is braising, a slow cooking method that allows spices to be added at various stages, resulting in well-rounded, layered flavours. Some curries rely on a combination of cooking techniques, such as marinating, frying and then roasting. None of these stages is difficult, and often some of them can be done in advance, making life easier for the cook. This ease of preparation and versatility partly account for the success of curry throughout the world, while the magic and intrigue of its spicing mean that one need never get bored. There are hundreds of variations for each dish – a minor nuance changed here or there can create something entirely different.

REGIONAL AND RELIGIOUS INFLUENCES

Far more important than learning recipes is to understand the context in which they developed. It is the context that gives them their soul. In India, region and religion have both had a big impact on the way in which the cuisine has developed.

The majority of the population in India is Hindu and does not eat beef, which is considered sacred. The second most commonly practised religion is Islam, which forbids the consumption of pork. It is because of these two restrictions that you don't often see pork and beef used in curries.

In Punjab, Kashmir and the north of the country, the climate is moderate to cold, while the soil is fertile and wheat is the staple grain, Vegetables and fruit grow in abundance and dairy produce is widely used. In this land of plenty, rich dishes made with milk, butter, lamb and chicken are common. The spicing varies a fair bit; dishes range from creamy butter chicken to rustic, hot, kadhai-style stir-fries, essentially relying on a basic combination of woody spices such as cumin, coriander, cardamom, cinnamon, star anise and cloves. The majority of the population is either Hindu or Muslim, so beef and pork are rarely seen.

In the eastern part of the country, the picture is very different. In Bengal rice is the staple rather than wheat, mustard oil is commonly used for cooking, and the spicing is fairly basic: onion seeds, fennel seeds, carom, mustard seeds, cumin and cardamom being the most common, with few of the more aromatic spices, such as star anise and saffron, ever making an appearance. The Bengalis' love of good food, however, is apparent in the multitude of fish and seafood dishes, which are so different from anywhere else in the country.

As a Communist state, West Bengal is one of only two states in India (Kerala being the other) where it is legal to buy and sell beef. This, together with the British influence during the days of the Raj, means that beef and pork are frequently seen on menus here.

The southern end of the peninsula, consisting of Andhra Pradesh, Tamil Nadu, Kerala and Karnataka, is blessed by a long coastline, and hence a strong bias towards seafood dishes. The population is a mix of all religions and every kind of dish is found, even pork. Rice is the staple in this region and spices are plentiful. So is coconut, and both the oil and the milk are used freely in cooking. The climate is quite tropical and can be very hot and humid. Chillies and spices are added liberally to dishes in order to promote sweating, creating a cooling effect.

On the western coast are Mumbai and Goa – one a melting pot of different cultures and culinary styles, the other a former Portuguese colony with strong European influences. While in Mumbai anything goes, and the food is a heady mix of Maharashtrian, Pan-Indian and world cuisine, Goa is synonymous with fresh seafood cooked with vibrant, bold spicing – very much like the spirit of its residents.

Further west, Gujarat and Rajasthan are predominantly vegetarian, although Rajasthan also has a tradition of cooking with game. Since much of the land is dry and arid, not much grows there and the vegetarian cuisine displays great innovation, with spicy, earthy flavours.

CURRY IN BRITAIN

In the UK, far from the land of its birth and the influences that shaped it, curry is a six-billion-pound industry. Between restaurants, takeaways and supermarkets, a vast amount of curry is sold on a daily basis. For years I believed that the longstanding British love affair with India was the reason Indian food was so popular here. To be honest, I'm now beginning to wonder if it's the other way round!

The British experience of curry has come a long way since the days when it was made with sultanas and curry powder. As more Asians have become part of British society, many people have had the opportunity to eat in their homes and discover genuine Indian food.

Restaurants have become more sophisticated and it is quite common now for them to specialise in regional food from various parts of India. At the same time, a genuinely British-Indian strand of cooking has developed. Much as top Indian chefs might turn up their noses at the typical high-street curry house, an entire generation of British people has grown up with Sylheti kormas, vindaloos and Madras curry and wouldn't have it any other way. I tried jhalfrezi for the first time when I arrived in London and also had my first balti in Birmingham – an experience,

to say the least. It was not something I had ever eaten in India but there were several people around me who were completely at ease with the dishes.

Anyone who has ever had a curry understands how addictive it can be, creating a craving for more. The pleasure sensations associated with eating curry come from the release of endorphins, and are known to drive many of us in the UK straight to a curry house when we come back from a holiday abroad. Little wonder, then, that when British officers returned from the subcontinent back in the days of the East India Company, they would bring sacks of spices, and sometimes even their own cooks, in order to be able to enjoy curries at home.

When I first travelled outside India – and particularly when I came to England – my eyes were opened to a phenomenon I had not known existed. The huge community of Indians living abroad, many of them over several generations, had invented new dishes, or adapted traditional curries to suit local ingredients. This new style of Indian food fused with the local cuisine to create an entirely different way of cooking. The results may be frowned upon by people back in India as inauthentic. But the question is, who decides what is authentic?

AUTHENTIC CURRY – YOURS OR MINE?

I recently met a Bori Muslim lady who has lived in Britain for 50 years but whose family originally came from Gujarat. Before they moved to Britain, three generations of her family had lived in East Africa over the course of a century. Effectively, the cooking in this family still drew from traditional Gujarati dishes but has adapted to include local, seasonal ingredients available in their new homes. A slow but constant evolution over 150 years has unquestionably changed their food and eating habits, but try telling this lady that the food she cooks for her family is not authentic!

If authentic cooking comes from the home, then there is no such thing as authentic Indian food, as no two homes ever cook a dish in exactly the same way. The search for authenticity is pointless, since what is the genuine article to me might mean nothing to you, and what is authentic today may be meaningless tomorrow.

Over the last 14 years as a chef, I have on numerous occasions seen authenticity used as an excuse for not doing things rather than the other way round. During the early days of The Cinnamon Club, guests would often tell me that they had loved their meal but weren't sure if they could call it authentic. My response would be, did it matter, as long as they had enjoyed it?

As Masaharu Morimoto describes in his book, *Morimoto: The New Art of Japanese Cooking* (DK Publishing, 2007), he experienced the same confusion in response to his cooking in the USA, which draws inspiration from traditional Japanese cuisine but also uses local produce and influences. His answer to the question of authenticity is: why isn't my food Japanese and why must it be?

I couldn't agree more. So many cuisines are merging and moulding, mixing and changing every day. Very few chefs' larders are restricted to what's local any more and in theory anything goes. Curry, like everything else, is subject to a continual process of change, evolving in order to remain accessible, popular and relevant.

This isn't only a recent phenomenon. It may sound blasphemous to say that the tandoor does not belong to India, or that the lovely naan bread we are all so used to ordering in Indian restaurants is not really Indian either, but that is the truth. In the mid-fifteenth century, when Mughal rulers invaded India from Persia via Afghanistan, they brought over many of their culinary influences, including the tandoor. Over the next few hundred years, these gradually blended in with local traditions. Today it has become almost impossible to identify and separate the different influences. And to be honest, why bother?

Tradition is nothing but successful innovation, and innovation today forms the basis of tradition tomorrow. Innovation draws from tradition, as it should. In terms of cooking curries, a sound, deep-rooted understanding of spices and techniques is fundamental to any successful innovation. Part of the joy of cooking at The Cinnamon Club is that I have the opportunity to deconstruct traditional curries into their essential parts and then build them up again, creating layers of flavour and texture and maximising the appreciation of the core ingredients. It's impossible to do this without a deep understanding of traditional dishes.

This book is an attempt to present curry in both its forms – classic and contemporary. It shows what curry has always been and what it could become. It is a celebration of the timeless nature of curry – a tradition that dates back centuries, yet remains popular today. While you will find in its pages some of the greatest recipes from all over the subcontinent, I hope you will also be inspired to create your own modern classics, adapting the recipes to suit your own tastes.

VIVEK SINGH, SEPTEMBER 2008

VEGETARIAN

BABY AUBERGINES WITH SESAME AND TAMARIND SAUCE

BAGHARE BAINGAN

There are different versions of this dish all over the country but the most popular one is from Hyderabad. It has rich, deep, earthy notes, and some recipes use fat green chillies alongside the aubergines, or even include lamb's liver in the sauce.

The term *baghare* refers to the tempering of the aubergines.

SERVES 4

12 baby aubergines
1½ teaspoons salt
2 tablespoons vegetable or corn oil
½ teaspoon mustard seeds
2 sprigs of fresh curry leaves
2 teaspoons Ginger-Garlic Paste (see page 202)
1 quantity of Boiled Onion Paste (see page 203)
¼ teaspoon ground turmeric
1 teaspoon red chilli powder
4 tablespoons tamarind paste
500ml (2 cups) water

For the masala paste
50g (½ cup) desiccated coconut
1 tablespoon peanuts
1 tablespoon sesame seeds
1 tablespoon coriander seeds
½ teaspoon cumin seeds
3 green chillies, chopped
2 tablespoons coriander stalks

To finish
a pinch of sugar
a sprig of mint, finely chopped
1 tablespoon Crisp Fried Onions (see page 203)

Make 2 deep slits in each aubergine, forming a cross from the base towards the stalk end but leaving the quarters attached. Leave the calyx and a little of the stalk on to hold the aubergine together. Sprinkle the aubergines with half the salt and set aside for a good 20 minutes.

Meanwhile, make the masala paste. Separately roast the coconut, peanuts, sesame, coriander and cumin seeds in a dry frying pan over a medium heat for a minute or two, then remove from the heat. Blitz them in a small food processor with the chillies and coriander stalks, adding just enough water to make a paste.

To cook the aubergines, heat 1 tablespoon of the oil in a large, heavy-based pan and fry them over a high heat for 2–3 minutes, stirring from time to time, until they are seared on all sides. Remove the aubergines from the pan and heat the remaining oil in it. Add the mustard seeds and curry leaves, let them crackle, then add the ginger-garlic paste and fry for 2–3 minutes, stirring constantly to prevent sticking. Add the onion paste and cook, stirring, until it turns light brown. Stir in the turmeric, red chilli powder and masala paste, reduce the heat and fry for 10–12 minutes, until the oil begins to separate from the mixture at the side of the pan. Now add the remaining salt and the tamarind paste and cook for 3–4 minutes.

Return the fried aubergines to the pan and mix well. Pour in the water and simmer for 10–12 minutes, until the aubergines are soft but still hold their shape. Finish with the sugar, chopped mint and fried onion. Serve with rice or Layered Parathas (see page 196).

Cook's note
Don't stir the aubergines too vigorously when simmering them in the sauce, as they break quite easily.

SEARED AUBERGINE STEAKS WITH SESAME TAMARIND SAUCE

This is a modern version of the previous recipe. Essentially it uses a Hyderabadi-style sauce but the aubergines are fried separately rather than cooked in the sauce. This technique is commonly seen in Bengal, while the spice mix is an adaptation of a housewives' recipe from the hills in Nainital. All in all, the dish uses techniques from various parts of India and combines the flavours beautifully.

SERVES 4

2 large aubergines
1 teaspoon salt
1/2 teaspoon ground turmeric
1/2 teaspoon red chilli powder
1 teaspoon fennel seeds
1/2 teaspoon black onion seeds
2 tablespoons gram (chickpea) flour
2 tablespoons rice flour
3 tablespoons vegetable or corn oil

For the stuffing
2 teaspoons fennel seeds, roasted in a
    dry frying pan and then coarsely
    pounded
1 teaspoon ground cumin
2 teaspoons ground coriander
3 teaspoons dried mango powder
1 teaspoon red chilli powder
1/2 teaspoon ground turmeric
1/2 teaspoon salt
1/4 teaspoon sugar
1/2 teaspoon black onion seeds
1/2 teaspoon carom seeds

For the sauce
2 tablespoons coriander seeds
1 tablespoon sesame seeds
1 teaspoon cumin seeds
50g (1/2 cup) desiccated coconut

4 tablespoons vegetable or corn oil
50g (1/2 cup) peanuts or cashew nuts
500ml (2 cups) water
4 dried red chillies
1/2 teaspoon mustard seeds
1/2 teaspoon black onion seeds
2 sprigs of fresh curry leaves
3 tablespoons Boiled Onion Paste
    (see page 203)
1 teaspoon red chilli powder
1/2 teaspoon ground turmeric
2 tablespoons tamarind paste
1 teaspoon salt
1/2 teaspoon sugar
25g (1/2 cup) fresh coriander,
    chopped

Combine all the ingredients for the stuffing and set aside.

Slice the aubergines into rounds 2cm (3/4-inch) thick. Make an incision on the side of each 'steak' towards the centre, then insert a small, sharp knife and make a pocket by turning the knife around. Fill the pockets with the dry spice stuffing, then rub the salt, turmeric, chilli powder, fennel seeds and black onion seeds over the outside. Set aside for 30 minutes to remove excess moisture.

For the sauce, roast the coriander, sesame and cumin seeds in a dry frying pan over a medium heat for a minute or so. Tip them out on to a plate and set aside. Roast the coconut in the same pan until golden, then add to the seeds. Heat a tablespoon of the oil in the pan, add the nuts and fry until golden. Put them in a

food processor with the seeds and coconut, add the water and blend to a smooth paste.

Heat the remaining oil in a pan, add the red chillies and mustard seeds and let them crackle. Add the onion seeds and curry leaves, followed by the onion paste, and cook for 8–10 minutes, until the oil separates from the mixture. Now add the ground seed and nut paste and stir over a low heat for a couple of minutes. Add the chilli powder, turmeric and tamarind paste and cook gently for 15–18 minutes, until the sauce thickens. Stir in the salt, sugar and coriander, then remove from the heat and keep warm.

To cook the aubergine, mix together the gram flour and rice flour and use to dust the steaks. Heat the 3 tablespoons of oil in a large frying pan, add the aubergines and fry over a medium heat for about 1 1/2 minutes on each side, until golden brown and cooked through.

Divide the sauce between 4 serving plates and put the aubergine steaks on top. Serve with steamed rice, garnished with Tapioca Crisps (see page 190).

SEARED BOTTLE GOURD WITH CHICKPEA BREAD AND BOTTLE GOURD COOKED IN MILK

This was inspired by a dish on the menu at The Cinnamon Club called aubergine cooked three ways. I was toying with the idea of serving slices of bottle gourd filled with paneer and spices when I stumbled across this amazing bottle gourd curry cooked slowly in milk with curry leaves. The textures were superb and it had all the richness I was looking for, so I decided simply to fry some bottle gourd slices to provide another texture. The combination of rich bottle gourd curry with chickpea bread is also an absolute winner.

SERVES 4

For the chickpea bread
150g (1 cup) gram (chickpea) flour
100g ($^2/_3$ cup) plain flour
1 teaspoon salt
1cm ($^1/_2$-inch) piece of fresh ginger, chopped
1 green chilli, finely chopped
1 tablespoon chopped fresh coriander
$^1/_2$ teaspoon carom seeds
$^1/_2$ teaspoon red chilli powder
$^1/_4$ teaspoon ground turmeric
1 red onion, chopped
1 spring onion, chopped
1 tablespoon vegetable or corn oil
100ml (scant $^1/_2$ cup) water
2 tablespoons ghee or butter

For the seared bottle gourd
500g (1lb 2oz) bottle gourd, peeled and
  cut into slices 1cm ($^1/_2$ inch) thick
$^1/_2$ teaspoon ground turmeric
$^1/_2$ teaspoon red chilli powder
$^1/_2$ teaspoon fennel seeds
$^1/_2$ teaspoon black onion seeds
1 teaspoon salt
2 tablespoons vegetable or corn oil
juice of $^1/_2$ lime

For the bottle gourd curry
2 tablespoons vegetable or corn oil
$^1/_2$ teaspoon mustard seeds
1 dried red chilli
10 fresh curry leaves
1 onion, chopped
1cm ($^1/_2$-inch) piece of fresh ginger,
  chopped
4 green chillies, slit open lengthwise
500g (1lb 2oz) bottle gourd, peeled
  and cut into 5mm ($^1/_4$-inch) dice
$^1/_2$ teaspoon ground turmeric
1 teaspoon salt
250ml (1 cup) milk
juice of $^1/_2$ lime
1 tablespoon chopped fresh
  coriander

For the sauce
4 tablespoons canned tomato purée
2 tablespoons butter
3 tablespoons single cream
$^1/_2$ teaspoon salt
$^1/_2$ teaspoon red chilli powder
a pinch of sugar
a pinch of dried fenugreek leaves

To make the bread dough, mix the gram flour and plain flour together in a bowl, then take out 3 tablespoons of the mixture and set aside for dusting. Add all the rest of the ingredients except the ghee and knead to make a stiff dough. Cover with a damp cloth and leave to rest for about 20 minutes.

Rub the bottle gourd slices with the spices and salt and set aside for about 20 minutes to remove excess moisture.

To make the bottle gourd curry, heat the oil in a saucepan and add the mustard seeds, dried chilli and curry leaves. When they crackle, add the onion and sauté until soft. Add the ginger and green chillies, followed by the bottle gourd, turmeric and salt, and sauté for a minute. Add half the milk, reduce the heat and cook, stirring occasionally, for 6–8 minutes, until the sauce thickens. Add the rest of the milk and continue cooking for about 10 minutes, till the bottle gourd is thoroughly tender. Squeeze the lime juice over, sprinkle in the coriander, then remove from the heat and keep warm.

Divide the bread dough into 4 pieces and shape them into balls. On a lightly floured surface, roll out each one into a circle about 15cm (6 inches) in diameter, dusting with the flour you set aside. Heat a large, non-stick frying pan or a flat griddle over a high heat and place a piece of dough on it. Cook for 3–4 minutes, until lightly browned underneath, then turn over and cook the other side. Reduce the heat, brush the top of the bread with some of the ghee or butter, then turn it over and cook until the colour has deepened. Brush the top again and repeat the process. Cook the remaining breads in the same way and keep warm. Clean out the pan with a dry kitchen cloth and heat the 2 tablespoons of oil for the seared bottle gourd in it. Remove any excess moisture from the bottle gourd slices with kitchen paper and place

them in the pan. Cook over a medium heat for 2–3 minutes, turning once, until they are just tender. Remove from the heat and squeeze the lime juice over.

For the sauce, put the tomato purée, butter and cream in a small pan and bring to the boil. Season with the salt, red chilli powder and sugar, then add the fenugreek.

To serve, pour the sauce on to 4 shallow plates or dishes and arrange the fried bottle gourd on top. Serve with the bottle gourd curry and chickpea bread.

Cook's notes
You could use wax gourd or another member of the marrow family instead of bottle gourd.

Any of the components of this dish would be very good on its own.

PUNJABI CHICKPEA FRITTERS IN YOGHURT CURRY

KADHI PAKORA

This is a firm favourite in most North Indian households. There are numerous versions of it, including ones from the Punjab, Rajasthan, Gujarat, Bengal-Orissa and Uttar Pradesh. The recipe below most closely resembles those from Uttar Pradesh.

I love this dish for its simplicity. It uses very basic ingredients yet there is an interesting play of textures and flavours. In a restaurant set-up, the kadhi is incredibly versatile and can easily be transformed into a soup or a sauce.

SERVES 4

For the yoghurt kadhi
500g (2 cups) plain yoghurt
2 tablespoons gram (chickpea) flour
600ml ($2\frac{1}{2}$ cups) water
$1\frac{1}{2}$ teaspoons salt
1 teaspoon ground turmeric
2 tablespoons ghee
2 dried red chillies
1 teaspoon cumin seeds
a sprig of fresh curry leaves
juice of 1 lemon

For the pakoras
4 red onions, thinly sliced
4 green chillies, finely chopped
$\frac{1}{2}$ teaspoon carom seeds
1 teaspoon red chilli powder
1 teaspoon salt
2.5cm (1-inch) piece of fresh ginger, finely chopped
10 large spinach leaves, finely shredded
1 tablespoon finely chopped fresh coriander
2 tablespoons gram (chickpea) flour
vegetable or corn oil for deep-frying

Start with the yoghurt kadhi. Whisk together the yoghurt, gram flour, water, salt and turmeric and pass through a fine sieve to get rid of any lumps. Place the mixture in a saucepan and bring to the boil over a medium heat, whisking constantly. Reduce the heat and simmer for 8–10 minutes, until it turns glossy and thickens enough to coat the back of a wooden spoon lightly. Skim off any scum or impurities that may have come to the surface. In a small pan, heat the ghee to smoking point. Add the dried chillies, cumin seeds and curry leaves and leave for a few seconds, until they splutter and crackle. Tip the contents of the pan over the yoghurt mixture and set aside.

Mix together all the ingredients for the pakoras except the flour and oil and set aside for 10 minutes or so, to allow the salt to draw out moisture from the onions and spinach. Sprinkle with the flour and mix lightly until the mixture just holds together.

In a large saucepan or a deep-fat fryer, heat the oil to 170°C/325°F. Drop in dessertspoonfuls of the batter to form small dumplings. Fry for 3–4 minutes, until crisp and golden, then drain on kitchen paper.

Bring the yoghurt kadhi back to the boil and drop the crisp fritters into it. Serve immediately, accompanied by steamed rice.

CHICKPEA POLENTA IN YOGHURT SAUCE

PITHOD KI SUBZI

Found only in Rajasthan, this is a very unusual vegetarian dish with yoghurt and gram flour as the primary ingredients. The technique is quite similar to that of set polenta or semolina gnocchi, and the combination of an unusual texture with a complex mix of spices provides a very interesting experience. This dish is good for the summer months and is best served with steamed rice.

SERVES 6

750g (3 cups) Greek-style yoghurt
500ml (2 cups) water
100g ($^2/_3$ cup) gram (chickpea) flour
1 teaspoon salt
$^1/_2$ teaspoon ground turmeric
$^1/_2$ teaspoon sugar
$^1/_2$ teaspoon garam masala
2.5cm (1-inch) piece of fresh ginger, finely chopped
2 tablespoons ghee
1 teaspoon fennel seeds
a pinch of asafoetida
vegetable or corn oil for frying

For the yoghurt sauce
2 tablespoons vegetable or corn oil
a pinch of asafoetida
1$^1/_2$ teaspoons cumin seeds
4 cloves
1 onion, finely chopped
400g (1$^2/_3$ cups) Greek-style yoghurt
2 tablespoons ground coriander
$^1/_2$ teaspoon ground turmeric
$^1/_2$ teaspoon red chilli powder
1 teaspoon salt
2 green chillies, slit lengthwise into quarters
200ml (scant 1 cup) water
a pinch of sugar (optional)

1cm ($^1/_2$-inch) piece of fresh ginger, cut into fine strips
20g ($^1/_2$ cup) fresh coriander, chopped
juice of $^1/_2$ lemon

Whisk the yoghurt and water with the gram flour, salt, turmeric, sugar, garam masala and ginger, then set aside. Heat the ghee in a large, heavy-based pan, add the fennel seeds and sauté briefly, then add the asafoetida and stir for 30 seconds. As the flavours are released, add the yoghurt mixture and cook over a medium heat, stirring constantly, for 20–25 minutes, until the mixture thickens and acquires the consistency of a soft dough. Remove from the heat and transfer to a greased 15cm (6-inch) square baking tin. Chill for about 30 minutes, until set like a cake.

To make the sauce, heat the oil in a saucepan over a moderate heat and add the asafoetida, cumin and cloves. When they begin to crackle, add the onion and cook gently for 8–10 minutes, until soft but not coloured. Whisk the yoghurt with the ground coriander, turmeric, chilli powder and salt. Add to the onion, stirring constantly, and keep stirring until the mixture comes to the boil; this will prevent the yoghurt splitting. Add the green chillies and water, bring back to the boil and simmer for about 5 minutes. Check the seasoning, adding more salt and the sugar to balance the taste if required. Stir in the ginger, fresh coriander and lemon juice and

keep warm.
Cut the gram flour 'cake' into 2.5cm (1-inch) squares. Heat a thin layer of oil in a large frying pan and add the squares a few at a time. Fry for a couple of minutes, until the outside gets a golden brown crust, then turn and cook the other side. Serve the fritters on top of the hot sauce, or mix them into the sauce and bring to a simmer before serving.

Variation
POPPADOM CURRY
(PAPAD KI SUBZI)

This imaginative use of the humble poppadom is unique to Rajasthan. Simply make the sauce as above, then cut 6 poppadoms into strips 2.5cm (1 inch) wide and simmer them in the sauce for 30 seconds–1 minute. Serve with Pilau Rice (see page 180).

CHICKPEA DUMPLINGS IN YOGHURT SAUCE

GATTE KI SUBZI

This Rajasthani dish symbolises austerity and creativity like no other. It is based on ingredients that are readily available in the dry, arid terrain of Rajasthan, where little else grows. By simply altering the proportions of these ingredients, the Rajasthanis have created a whole range of different dishes such as Kadhi Pakora (see page 23) and Pithod ki Subzi (see page 24).

These chickpea dumplings are a bit of an acquired taste for many people in the Western world but, as a curry that characterises the originality of Rajasthani vegetarian cuisine, it is quite unrivalled and thus deserves its place in this book.

SERVES 4

For the chickpea dumplings
250g (1²/₃ cups) gram (chickpea) flour
¹/₂ tablespoon finely chopped fresh ginger
2 green chillies, finely chopped
¹/₂ teaspoon ground turmeric
a pinch of asafoetida
¹/₂ teaspoon cumin seeds, roasted in a dry frying pan
2 pinches of carom seeds
a pinch of bicarbonate of soda
1 teaspoon finely chopped mint
125g (¹/₂ cup) Greek-style yoghurt, tied in a muslin cloth and left hanging up overnight to drain
2 teaspoons ghee
¹/₂ teaspoon salt
vegetable or corn oil for deep-frying

For the yoghurt sauce
250g (1 cup) plain yoghurt
¹/₂ teaspoon ground turmeric
¹/₂ teaspoon ground coriander
1 teaspoon red chilli powder
2.5cm (1-inch) piece of fresh ginger, finely chopped
1 teaspoon salt
1¹/₂ tablespoons ghee
1 bay leaf
2 dried red chillies
¹/₂ teaspoon cumin seeds
1 onion, finely chopped
2 green chillies, slit open lengthwise
1¹/₂ teaspoons dried fenugreek leaves
250ml (1 cup) water
1 teaspoon mint leaves

Mix together all the ingredients for the dumplings except the oil and knead well, adding a very little water to form a firm but pliable dough. Cover with cling film and set aside for 15 minutes.

Divide the dough into 8 pieces and shape them into cylinders about 1cm (¹/₂ inch) in diameter, rolling them on the worktop with the palm of your hand. Now cut them into batons 4cm (1¹/₂ inches) long. In a large saucepan or a deep-fat fryer, heat the oil to about 120–140°C. Add the dumplings and fry for 6–8 minutes, until golden. Drain on kitchen paper and set aside.

For the yoghurt sauce, whisk the yoghurt, turmeric, coriander, chilli powder, ginger and salt together, then set aside. Heat the ghee in a heavy-based pan over a high heat and add the bay leaf, dried chillies and cumin seeds. When they crackle, add the onion and reduce the heat. Cook gently until the onion is translucent, then pour in the yoghurt mixture. Stir continuously, gradually increasing the heat, until the yoghurt comes to the boil. On no account stop stirring, or the yoghurt will split.

When the yoghurt starts to boil, add the green chillies, fenugreek leaves and water and simmer for 2 minutes. Now add the dumplings and simmer for 6 minutes, until they are heated through and have soaked up some of the sauce to thicken it slightly. Take care to add the dumplings just before you are ready to serve; if you leave them in the sauce for too long, they tend to soak up too much liquid and break up. Scatter with the mint leaves and serve hot, with a bread of your choice or even steamed rice.

Cook's note

If you don't want to fry the dumplings, you could wrap the dough cylinders in foil and poach them in a pan of salted water for 12–15 minutes, then cut them into short lengths and finish cooking in the sauce, as above. This works just as well and is much healthier.

Left to right
Chickpea Dumplings in Yoghurt Sauce (page 25); Chickpea Polenta in Yoghurt Sauce (page 24);
Poppadom Curry (page 24).

WINTER VEGETABLE CURRY WITH CARROTS, PEAS AND TOMATOES

GAJJAR MUTTER TAMATAR KI SUBZI

This humble vegetable curry is cooked in almost every household in northern India. Generally considered too mundane to put on restaurant menus, it is an all-time favourite at home, and comes in many guises – made with cauliflower or turnips instead of the vegetables listed below, for example, or served with lots of sauce to accompany rice. If the water is omitted, this semi-dry dish goes down a treat with chapattis. I rather prefer the drier version, as the flavours are more pronounced.

SERVES 4

3 tablespoons vegetable or corn oil
1 bay leaf
4 green cardamom pods
1 teaspoon cumin seeds
3 onions, finely chopped
3 ripe tomatoes, blended to a purée
2.5cm (1-inch) piece of fresh ginger, finely chopped
2 green chillies, cut lengthwise in half
$1/2$ teaspoon ground turmeric
$1/2$ teaspoon red chilli powder
1 teaspoon ground cumin
1 teaspoon ground coriander
2 teaspoons salt
4 carrots, peeled and cut into 1cm ($1/2$-inch) dice
200g ($1 1/3$ cups) peas
250ml (1 cup) water
juice of 1 lemon
2 tablespoons chopped fresh coriander or dill

Heat the oil in a heavy-based pan, add the bay leaf, cardamom pods and cumin seeds and let them crackle. Add the chopped onions and cook over a fairly high heat until golden brown. Stir in the puréed tomatoes, ginger, green chillies, spices and salt and cook for 8–10 minutes, until the oil begins to separate from the mixture at the sides of the pan. Add the carrots and cook, stirring, for 2 minutes, then add the peas and cook for 3 minutes. Pour in the water and cook till the vegetables are tender but still retain a little bite. Check the seasoning, then stir in the lemon juice and sprinkle with the chopped herbs. Serve hot with with chapattis or Naan Bread (see page 192).

Cook's note

If you cut the carrots even smaller, in 5mm ($1/4$-inch) dice, and cook the mixture without adding any water, then it could be used as a topping for various canapés or as a filling for wraps (made using supermarket tortillas, if you like). Papdi – wheat crisps, available in Indian supermarkets – topped with this vegetable curry make a good canapé option.

HOME-STYLE CURRY OF POTATOES AND CAULIFLOWER

ALOO GOBHI

This is probably the most common and basic vegetable curry you will find anywhere in India. Cooked pretty much nine months of the year, it is one of those recipes that sparks an intense debate over authenticity. One of the disadvantages of its universal appeal is that there is no such thing as a universal recipe!

SERVES 4

3 tablespoons vegetable or corn oil
1 teaspoon cumin seeds
1 large onion, chopped
1 tablespoon Ginger-Garlic Paste
  (see page 202)
4 green chillies, slit open lengthwise
2 medium potatoes, peeled and cut into
  2.5cm (1-inch) dice
1 cauliflower, divided into florets
1 teaspoon ground turmeric
2 teaspoons salt
2 tomatoes, chopped
$1/2$ teaspoon garam masala
1 tablespoon chopped fresh coriander
5cm (2-inch) piece of fresh ginger, cut
  into fine strips
juice of $1/2$ lime

Heat the oil in a wide, shallow pan and add the cumin seeds, followed by the onion. Sauté for about 5 minutes, until the onion is soft, then add the ginger-garlic paste and fry for a few seconds longer. Add the green chillies and potatoes and sauté over a high heat for a couple of minutes. Tip in the cauliflower, turmeric and salt, mix well, then reduce the heat. Cover the pan and cook for about 10 minutes, stirring occasionally to prevent sticking.

Add the tomatoes and garam masala and cook for about 5 minutes, until the vegetables are completely tender. Sprinkle in the chopped coriander and the ginger, squeeze over the lime juice and serve – either with chapattis or as a side dish.

Cook's notes
If you cut the cauliflower florets slightly bigger than the potatoes, they will cook in roughly the same time, rather than overcooking and disintegrating before the potatoes are done.

It's important to use a wide, shallow pan for this dish. If you use a deep pan or a wok instead, don't overcrowd it with the vegetables or they will start to disintegrate.

STIR-FRIED OKRA

A home-style stir-fry of okra, often cooked in North Indian homes in the rainy season when okra is abundant. It's a very simple dish but can be tricky to get right. If the okra is not dried properly after washing, or you add any water during cooking, it can become quite slimy and sticky. Many people don't like okra because they think it will be slimy, but cooked right it's a thing of beauty!

SERVES 4

6 tablespoons vegetable or corn oil
2 teaspoons cumin seeds
$^{1}/_{2}$ teaspoon fenugreek seeds
2 red onions, finely chopped
800g (1$^{3}/_{4}$lb) okra, topped and tailed,
    then sliced into 1cm ($^{1}/_{2}$-inch) rounds
1 teaspoon ground cumin
1 teaspoon ground coriander
1 teaspoon red chilli powder
1 tomato, deseeded and cut into 1cm
    ($^{1}/_{2}$-inch) dice
3cm (1$^{1}/_{4}$-inch) piece of fresh ginger,
    finely chopped
1$^{1}/_{2}$ teaspoons salt
1 teaspoon dried mango powder
$^{1}/_{2}$ teaspoon garam masala (optional)

Heat the oil in a wide frying pan over a medium heat and add the cumin and fenugreek seeds. When they start to crackle, add the onions and fry until golden brown. Add the okra and cook over a fairly high heat for 6–8 minutes, until it is crisp and the juices have dried up. Add the ground cumin, coriander and chilli powder and cook, stirring occasionally, for 2 minutes. Now add the tomato and toss quickly over a high heat. Stir in the ginger, salt and mango powder. For an extra touch of flavour, add the garam masala, then serve immediately.

Cook's note
Stir as little as possible after adding the okra, otherwise the juices will make the dish slimy. The salt is added after the okra has dried up, as it draws out the juices. Plenty of oil and a high heat ensure that the okra becomes crisp.

OMELETTE CURRY

This rather simple dish, made with rolled-up spiced omelette, is quick and easy, yet impressive. You can be really imaginative with the flavourings and try whatever is in season. Serve as a main dish or an accompaniment.

SERVES 4

6 free-range hen or duck eggs
1 red onion, finely chopped
2 green chillies, deseeded and finely
   chopped
$^1/_2$ teaspoon cumin seeds, roasted in a dry
   frying pan and then coarsely crushed
$^1/_2$ teaspoon ground turmeric
1 tablespoon finely chopped chives
1 teaspoon finely chopped fresh
   coriander
$1^1/_2$ teaspoons salt
1cm ($^1/_2$-inch) piece of fresh ginger,
   finely chopped
2 tablespoons vegetable or corn oil

For the sauce
3 tablespoons vegetable or corn oil
2 green cardamom pods
1 bay leaf
1 large onion, finely chopped
1 tablespoon Ginger-Garlic Paste
   (see page 202)
1 teaspoon red chilli powder
$^1/_2$ teaspoon ground cumin
$^1/_2$ teaspoon ground coriander
$^1/_2$ teaspoon ground turmeric
1 teaspoon salt
3 ripe tomatoes, puréed
$^1/_2$ teaspoon sugar
$^1/_2$ teaspoon garam masala
1 tablespoon chopped fresh coriander
1 tablespoon single cream
juice of $^1/_2$ lemon

Break the eggs into a bowl and whisk them lightly with all the other ingredients except the oil. Heat the oil in a large, non-stick frying pan and pour in just enough egg mix to make a thin omelette. Cook, without stirring, over a medium-high heat until it begins to set, then remove from the pan (without turning it over) and roll into a cylinder, like a swiss roll. Repeat with the remaining egg mix. Cut the omelette rolls in slices 1.5cm ($^2/_3$ inch) thick and keep warm.

For the sauce, heat the oil in a pan, add the green cardamom and bay leaf and let them crackle for 30 seconds or so. Add the onion and cook until golden brown. Add the ginger-garlic paste and stir for a minute. Add the red chilli powder, cumin, coriander, turmeric and salt and cook for another minute or so. Stir in the puréed tomatoes and cook for 6–8 minutes, until the mixture has reduced by half. Add the sugar and garam masala, then finish with the fresh coriander, single cream and lemon juice.

Pour the sauce into a serving dish and arrange the omelette slices on top. Serve immediately.

Cook's note
You could add finely chopped raw vegetables, such as asparagus, spinach or artichokes, to the beaten egg if you like. Or experiment with the sauce, adding curry leaves and coconut milk if you want to make it more interesting.

GREEN MOONG TADKA WITH SCRAMBLED EGG

In Punjab and the rest of northern India, the term *tadka* refers to tempering cumin, chillies, onions, etc., before using them to finish lentils and similar dishes. The final addition of spices cooked in hot ghee gives them smokiness and a pronounced kick. In roadside cafés along the highways of eastern India, the meaning has become distorted, and *tadka* refers to a dish of green moong lentils. I've seen many variations of this lentil dish, some with a sauce made from chicken, lamb or even egg. This version uses egg.

SERVES 4

200g (1 cup) whole green moong lentils
2.5 litres (2¹/₂ quarts) water
1 tablespoon salt
1 tablespoon Ginger-Garlic Paste
 (see page 202)
1 bay leaf
3 black cardamom pods
4 tablespoons vegetable or corn oil
1 teaspoon cumin seeds
1 tablespoon chopped garlic
2 onions, very finely chopped
1¹/₂ teaspoons chilli powder
1 tablespoon ground coriander
3 very ripe tomatoes, puréed
2–3 green chillies, finely chopped
¹/₂ teaspoon garam masala
1 tablespoon butter
juice of ¹/₂ lemon
4 free-range eggs, lightly beaten
1 tablespoon chopped fresh coriander

Wash the lentils, leave them to soak in cold water for 20 minutes, then drain. Put them in a pan with the water, three-quarters of the salt, plus the ginger-garlic paste, bay leaf and black cardamom pods. Bring to the boil and simmer for about 50 minutes, until the lentils are soft but still hold their shape.

Heat 2 tablespoons of the oil in a large, heavy-based pan and add the cumin seeds. When they crackle, add the garlic and fry until golden. Add three-quarters of the onions and cook till golden brown, then stir in the chilli powder and ground coriander. Cook for 3–5 minutes, until the oil starts to separate from the mixture round the edge of the pan. Add the puréed tomatoes and cook for 8–10 minutes. Pour the boiled lentils into this mixture, bring to the boil and simmer for 10–12 minutes. Add the green chillies and garam masala and cook gently until the onion mix and lentils are thoroughly combined and the lentils thicken the mix slightly so it is homogenous. Simmer for another 2–3 minutes, then add the butter and lemon juice. Transfer to a serving bowl.

Heat the remaining oil in a separate pan and sauté the remaining onion in it until translucent. Add the eggs and the remaining salt and cook gently, stirring to scramble the eggs. Pour the eggs over the lentils. Garnish with the coriander and serve hot, accompanied by Layered Parathas (see page 196) or Naan Bread (see page 192).

Cook's note
If you like, you could extend any leftover chicken or lamb curry by adding plain boiled green moong lentils to it and heating through thoroughly.

PUNJABI SPICED CHICKPEAS

PINDI CHOLEY

This classic Punjabi dish is also prepared with minor variations in Pakistan, Delhi and almost the entire north of India. Traditionally served with deep-fried leavened breads called *bhaturey*, it is just as good with steamed rice or served with tamarind chutney as part of *chaats* – a variety of tangy, sweet and sour mixes sold as street snacks in northern India.

Pindi choley refers to a rich, dark and earthy preparation of chickpeas in Rawalpindi style. *Pind* also refers to a Punjabi word for village, making this dish 'village-style chickpeas'. The characteristic colour comes from boiling the chickpeas in tin containers with the addition of dried gooseberries. Some people cheat and use tealeaves to add colour.

My version here is slightly different and does not call for dried gooseberries, which are a bit of an acquired taste. Instead the sourness comes from dried pomegranate seeds, which serve the dual purpose of adding flavour as well as texture.

SERVES 4

200g (1 cup) chickpeas, soaked in plenty of cold water overnight
a pinch of bicarbonate of soda (optional)
6 tablespoons vegetable or corn oil
2 black cardamom pods
$1/2$ teaspoon cloves
2 bay leaves
1 teaspoon cumin seeds
$1/2$ teaspoon asafoetida
2 onions, finely chopped
1 tablespoon Ginger Paste (see page 202)
1 teaspoon Garlic Paste (see page 202)
3 tomatoes, finely chopped
3 green chillies, chopped
2 teaspoons salt
2 teaspoons red chilli powder
1 tablespoon ground coriander
1 teaspoon dried mango powder
1 tablespoon dried pomegranate seeds (*anardana*), coarsely pounded
1 teaspoon sugar
juice of 1 lemon
2 tablespoons chopped fresh coriander
2.5cm (1-inch) piece of fresh ginger, cut into fine strips

Drain the chickpeas, put them in a large, heavy-based pan and pour in 2–2.5 litres (2–2$1/2$ quarts) of water, or enough to cover the chickpeas generously. You could add a pinch of bicarbonate of soda to reduce the cooking time. Bring to the boil and simmer until the chickpeas are soft enough to give way when pressed between your fingers.

Heat the oil in a separate pan, add the cardamom pods, cloves and bay leaves and cook, stirring, over a high heat for 30 seconds. Add the cumin seeds and asafoetida and cook for 30–60 seconds, until the seeds crackle. Then add the onions and sauté for 6–8 minutes, until golden brown. Stir in the ginger and garlic pastes and sauté for another minute or two. Add the tomatoes and stir-fry them over a high heat for a couple of minutes. Add the green chillies and salt and cook for another 3 minutes. Add the chilli powder and ground coriander and cook for 6–8 minutes, until the mixture turns dark and the oil starts to separate round the edge of the pan.

Drain the chickpeas and add them to the pan. Using the back of a wooden spoon, mash a few chickpeas to thicken the gravy. Add the dried mango powder and crushed pomegranate seeds. Check the seasoning, add the sugar and lemon juice, then garnish with the coriander and ginger. Serve with steamed rice or bread.

Cook's notes

If you can't find dried pomegranate seeds, use 2–3 tablespoons of thick tamarind pulp instead; it works just as well.

If the water evaporates before the chickpeas are tender, add some boiling water from the kettle. It's always better to start with more water than you think will be necessary. Adding cold water to chickpeas just makes them tougher and they take forever to cook!

Rather than using dried chickpeas, you could substitute 2 drained cans of chickpeas.

MOREL MUSHROOM AND GREEN PEA CURRY
GUCHHI MUTTER

This is a once-in-a-while treat that would not be out of place in a five-star restaurant. Morels are extremely difficult to find in India and fresh ones are eaten only by wealthy families on very special occasions. You can use dried or fresh morels in this dish. When peas are in season, the delicate combination of morels with fresh peas is simply delightful. Otherwise, substitute frozen petits pois, which are very nearly as good.

SERVES 4–6

12–16 dried or fresh morel mushrooms
4 tablespoons vegetable oil or ghee
$^1/_4$ teaspoon royal (black) cumin seeds
3 green cardamom pods
1cm ($^1/_2$-inch) piece of cinnamon stick
2 onions, finely chopped
2.5cm (1-inch) piece of fresh ginger, chopped
3 garlic cloves, chopped
6 tomatoes, blended to a purée
$^1/_2$ teaspoon ground turmeric
1 teaspoon red chilli powder
1 teaspoon ground cumin
2 teaspoons salt
300g (2 cups) shelled fresh peas or frozen petits pois
2 tablespoons Crisp Fried Onions (see page 203)
3 tablespoons single cream
1 teaspoon finely chopped mint
$^1/_4$ teaspoon Mace and Cardamom Powder (see page 204)
a pinch of sugar (optional)
1 tablespoon butter

Soak the morels in warm water for 15 minutes (30 minutes if they are dried), then drain. Remove the stalks and wash the mushrooms in several changes of water to get rid of any sand or grit. Drain the mushrooms, dry them on kitchen paper and cut them into 2–4 pieces, depending on size. Set aside.

Heat the oil or ghee in a heavy-based pan and add the royal cumin, cardamom and cinnamon. Once they crackle and pop, add the onions and sauté over a moderate heat until golden brown. Add the ginger and garlic and sauté for 2–3 minutes, then add the puréed tomatoes, turmeric, chilli powder, ground cumin and salt. Cook over a medium heat for 10–12 minutes, until the oil starts separating from the mixture at the edge of the pan. Add the morels and sauté for 2 minutes, then add the peas and stir for a minute or so.

Add the fried onions, cream and chopped mint and mix well. Check the seasoning and stir in the mace and cardamom and a pinch of sugar, if necessary. Finally stir in the butter. Serve with Layered Parathas (see page 196) or any other bread.

Cook's note
It's impossible to say how long you should wash the morels. Just keep on washing them until all the grit and small particles have gone. If the morels are very small, it's better to cut them up before washing, as it will be easier to get rid of the dirt.

PANEER CHEESE IN CREAMY FENUGREEK SAUCE

PANEER METHI MALAI

This is one of several hundred paneer curries made in India. I find it interesting, as the combination of creamy paneer works very well with the fragrant, herbaceous fenugreek.

SERVES 4

100g (1 cup) fresh fenugreek leaves, chopped
4 tablespoons ghee or vegetable oil
$1/2$ teaspoon cumin seeds
$1/4$ teaspoon asafoetida
1 onion, finely chopped
2.5cm (1-inch) piece of fresh ginger, finely chopped
4 green chillies, slit open lengthwise
150g ($2/3$ cup) Boiled Cashew Paste (see page 202)
500g (1lb 2oz) paneer, cut into 1cm ($1/2$-inch) cubes
250ml (1 cup) whole milk
$1^1/2$ teaspoons salt
$1/2$ teaspoon sugar
125ml ($1/2$ cup) single cream
1 tablespoon dried fenugreek leaves
$1/2$ teaspoon Mace and Cardamom Powder (see page 204)
juice of $1/2$ lemon

Bring about 1 litre (4 cups) of salted water to the boil in a saucepan. Add the fresh fenugreek leaves and when the water returns to the boil, drain them immediately and refresh in iced water. Set aside.

Heat the ghee or oil in a heavy-based pan, add the cumin and asafoetida, then the onion, and cook, stirring, until the onion is light golden brown. Add the ginger and green chillies, followed by the cashew paste, and stir for 4–6 minutes. Add the paneer, then the milk, and cook over a medium heat for about 5 minutes. Stir in the salt and sugar, followed by the cream, the fresh and dried fenugreek leaves and the mace and cardamom. Heat through gently, then squeeze in the lemon juice and remove from the heat. Serve with Layered Parathas (see page 196) or Pilau Rice (see page 180).

Cook's note
Do not cook for too long after adding the fresh fenugreek or it will discolour the dish and make it taste bitter.

SPICED GRATED PANEER WITH PEPPERS

PANEER BHURJI

Paneer is probably one of the most popular vegetarian ingredients in India. It is generally cooked in a curry but this way of serving it as a crumble or moist mash is very versatile, lending itself to many different uses. You can spread it on bread, use it as a filling for a wrap, or even as a pizza topping. If you spread it on naan bread and cut it into squares, it makes an excellent yet simple canapé.

SERVES 4

3 tablespoons vegetable or corn oil
1 teaspoon cumin seeds
1 onion, chopped
2.5cm (1-inch) piece of fresh ginger, chopped
4 green chillies, chopped
$^1/_2$ teaspoon ground turmeric
$^1/_2$ red pepper, cut into 5mm ($^1/_4$-inch) dice
$^1/_2$ green pepper, cut into 5mm ($^1/_4$-inch) dice
$^1/_2$ yellow pepper, cut into 5mm ($^1/_4$-inch) dice
$1^1/_2$ teaspoons salt
$^1/_2$ teaspoon sugar
300g ($10^1/_2$oz) paneer, grated
1 tablespoon chopped fresh coriander
juice of $^1/_2$ lemon
2 tablespoons single cream (optional)

Heat the oil in a frying pan and add the cumin seeds, followed by the onion, ginger and green chillies. Sauté until the onion is soft. Add the turmeric, then the peppers, salt and sugar, and sauté for a minute. Stir in the paneer and mix well. Sprinkle the fresh coriander on top and squeeze in the lemon juice. If the mixture feels dry, fold in the cream. Remove from the heat and serve with Naan Bread (see page 192).

PANEER BUTTER MASALA

Similar to chicken tikka masala in the UK, paneer butter masala is the most famous and widely interpreted paneer dish in India. I learned this recipe from contract banquet cooks from Orissa, who cooked at my sister's wedding and prepared this dish for 1,200 people. Needless to say, I've scaled it down several hundred times!

SERVES 4

4 tablespoons ghee or vegetable oil
1/2 teaspoon cumin seeds
4 green cardamom pods
2 black cardamom pods
1 bay leaf
1 large onion, finely chopped
1 1/2 teaspoons salt
1/2 teaspoon ground white pepper
1 tablespoon Ginger-Garlic Paste
  (see page 202)
1 1/2 teaspoons red chilli powder
5 ripe tomatoes, puréed
2 tablespoons whole milk powder
1 tablespoon Greek-style yoghurt
1 tablespoon Boiled Cashew Paste (see
  page 202)
500g (1lb 2oz) paneer, cut into 2.5cm
  (1-inch) rounds or dice
1 tablespoon dried fenugreek leaves
1/2 teaspoon garam masala
1/2 teaspoon sugar
3 tablespoons single cream
25g (2 tablespoons) cold butter, cut into
  small dice
1 tablespoon chopped fresh coriander
juice of 1/2 lemon

Heat the ghee or oil in a large, heavy-based casserole, add the cumin seeds, green and black cardamom pods and bay leaf and let them crackle. Add the onion and sauté over a high heat for 4–5 minutes, stirring constantly to prevent the onion colouring. Add the salt, then reduce the heat, cover and cook for 10–12 minutes, allowing the onion to soften and reduce to bring out its natural sweetness. Stir in the white pepper, ginger-garlic paste and chilli powder and cook for another 5 minutes, stirring constantly. Now add the puréed tomatoes and cook gently for 10–12 minutes, until the tomatoes have reduced by half and the oil begins to separate from the mixture round the side of the pan. Add the milk powder and mix well, then stir in the yoghurt. Add the cashew paste and cook for 3–5 minutes. Add the paneer and cook, stirring, for a minute or so, taking care not to break it up. Stir in the dried fenugreek, garam masala and sugar, followed by the cream, and simmer for another minute or two. Finally stir in the cold butter, a few pieces at a time, to emulsify the sauce; be careful not to let it boil. Sprinkle with the fresh coriander, squeeze in the lemon and serve, accompanied by Pilau Rice (see page 180) or Layered Parathas (see page 196).

Cook's note
Cooking the onion on a slow heat with the lid on is the secret to getting a really lovely, silky, velvety sauce that is unique to Paneer Butter Masala. Take your time to get the onion right and you will enjoy the dish that much more.

PUNJABI-STYLE MUSTARD GREENS

SARSON KA SAAG

This rustic dish is a firm favourite in the winter months, when the fields in Punjab are filled with mustard and their greens are plentiful. The very mention of a rich mustard purée served with dollops of freshly churned homemade butter, jaggery and chickpea bread brings tears to Punjabi men's eyes!

SERVES 4

1 tablespoon vegetable or corn oil
1 small onion, sliced
1 turnip, roughly diced
$\frac{1}{2}$ carrot, roughly diced
2.5cm (1-inch) piece of fresh ginger, grated
2 garlic cloves, crushed
4 green chillies, slit open lengthwise
300g ($10\frac{1}{2}$oz) bunch of mustard greens (available in most Asian supermarkets), roughly chopped
100g ($3\frac{1}{2}$ oz) bunch of spinach, roughly chopped
1 teaspoon salt
$\frac{1}{2}$ teaspoon sugar

For the tempering
4 tablespoons mustard oil or vegetable oil
6 garlic cloves, chopped
1 onion, chopped
1 tablespoon cornmeal
50g ($\frac{1}{4}$ cup) unsalted butter
$\frac{1}{2}$ teaspoon garam masala
juice of $\frac{1}{2}$ lime

Heat the oil in a heavy-based pan, add the onion, then cover and sweat until soft. Add the turnip and carrot and sweat for 3–4 minutes, until half cooked. Add the ginger, garlic and green chillies and cook for another 3–4 minutes. Now add the mustard greens and spinach to the pot, sprinkle with 2 tablespoons of water and add the salt and sugar. Cover and cook over a low heat until the vegetables are completely cooked in their own steam. Remove from the heat and blend to a smooth purée in a food processor.

To prepare the tempering, heat the oil in a pan and add the garlic, followed by the onion. Sauté until the onion turns golden, then add the purée and stir over a high heat for 4–5 minutes, until the onion and purée are well mixed and the oil is just about to start separating from the mixture. Sprinkle in the cornmeal, mix well and cook for 3–4 minutes. Add the butter and garam masala and mix them in thoroughly. Squeeze the lime juice over and remove from the heat.

Serve hot, accompanied by Chickpea Bread (see page 20), butter and crushed jaggery.

Cook's note
This dish can be served in different guises, as little canapés on squares of bread, as a spread, or as a dip for finger food.

GUJARATI-STYLE SWEET AND SOUR MIXED VEGETABLES

DHAN SAAK

This is probably one of the most popular dishes in any high-street curry house in the UK. The recipe comes from the Parsee community of Mumbai and it may seem like a lot of work but, believe me, this is the real McCoy!

SERVES 4–6

50g (¼ cup) toor dal
50g (¼ cup) moong dal (split yellow mung beans)
25g (⅛ cup) urad dal (white urid lentils)
50g (¼ cup) masoor dal (red lentils)
25g (⅛ cup) chana dal (yellow split peas)
2 litres (8 cups) water
1 teaspoon ground turmeric
1½ teaspoons salt

For the dhan saak masala
4 dried red chillies
12 black peppercorns
⅛ nutmeg
8 cloves
¼ teaspoon fenugreek seeds
1 teaspoon sesame seeds
1 tablespoon garam masala

For the vegetables
1 small potato, peeled and diced
1 carrot, diced
1 small onion, diced
1 small aubergine, cut into 2.5cm (1-inch) dice
2 tomatoes, deseeded and diced
200g (7oz) spinach
75g (¾ cup) fresh fenugreek leaves
2 tablespoons coriander leaves
10–15 mint leaves
2 tablespoons grated fresh coconut
1 teaspoon salt
1.5 litres (6 cups) water

To finish
1 tablespoon vegetable or corn oil
1 tablespoon Ginger Paste (see page 202)
1 tablespoon Garlic Paste (see page 202)
4 tablespoons tamarind paste
500ml (2 cups) water

First make the dhan saak masala. Roast all the ingredients except the garam masala in a dry frying pan over a medium heat for a minute or so. Grind them in a spice grinder or coffee grinder, then stir in the garam masala and set aside.

Put all the pulses in a sieve and rinse them under cold running water until clean. Place in a heavy-based pan, add the water, turmeric and salt and bring to the boil. Simmer for ¾–1 hour, until the pulses are very tender. Blitz to a smooth paste in a food processor and set aside.

Put all the ingredients for the vegetables in a pan, bring to the boil, then reduce the heat and simmer until they are tender. Leave to cool, then purée the mixture in the pan, using a hand-held blender.

To finish the dish, heat the oil in a heavy-based pan and add the boiled pulses mixture. Cook over a high heat for 5 minutes, then add the ginger, garlic and tamarind pastes and cook for another 5 minutes, stirring all the while. Now add the puréed vegetables and keep on stirring for 6–8 minutes. Next stir in the dhan saak masala. When the masala is thoroughly incorporated, add the water. Correct the seasoning if required. Let the dhan saak cook for at least half an hour over a very low heat, stirring from time to time. When the mixture acquires the consistency of a thick sauce, remove from the heat. Serve with a chopped salad and rice (see notes below).

Cook's notes
Meat eaters could add pieces of chicken or meat after the masala and water have been added.

Traditionally Parsees prefer to let a little dhan saak stick to the bottom of the pan, which imparts a slightly burnt taste. If it gets too thick, however, add a little water.

Traditional accompaniments are *kachumbar* (a salad made of finely diced cucumber, tomato and onion seasoned with finely chopped coriander and mint leaves, along with a dash of vinegar, salt and pepper) and 'brown rice' (rice cooked with ¼ teaspoon of caramelised sugar to give it a light brown colour).

TAWA PALAK METHI MUSHROOM

Strictly speaking, this dish could be made in a kadhai, or Indian wok, rather than a tawa, but using a flat iron griddle increases the surface area and therefore makes the cooking much faster and more exciting.

You could add other ingredients to a simple dish like this, such as broccoli, cauliflower, peppers or paneer.

SERVES 4

250g (9oz) young spinach leaves
50g (1/2 cup) fresh fenugreek leaves
4 tablespoons vegetable or corn oil
2 dried chillies
1 teaspoon coriander seeds
1 teaspoon cumin seeds
3 garlic cloves, chopped
2 onions, finely chopped, plus 2 onions, thickly sliced
1/2 teaspoon ground turmeric
6 green chillies, finely chopped
2.5cm (1-inch) piece of fresh ginger, chopped
2 teaspoons ground cumin
1 teaspoon red chilli powder
1 teaspoon fennel seeds
6 tomatoes, chopped, plus 1 tomato, deseeded and cut into wedges
500g (1lb 2oz) chestnut mushrooms, cut in half, or quartered if large
2 teaspoons salt
250g (9oz) baby sweetcorn, cut lengthwise in half
2 teaspoons dried fenugreek leaves, crushed with your fingertips
juice of 1 lime

Wash the spinach leaves and fenugreek leaves separately to get rid of any earth or grit, then drain well. Roughly tear the spinach and set aside. Chop the fenugreek leaves roughly, discarding the stalks.

Heat the oil on a thick, heavy griddle pan and add the dried chillies, coriander seeds and cumin seeds. When they crackle, add the garlic and sauté until golden, then add the finely chopped onions and sauté until brown. Stir in the turmeric, green chillies, chopped ginger, cumin, chilli powder and fennel seeds and cook over a high heat for 2 minutes. Now add the chopped tomatoes and stir until the oil starts to separate from the mixture at the edge of the pan. Toss in the mushrooms over a high heat, add the salt and cook, stirring frequently, for 3 minutes. Add the baby sweetcorn and the thickly sliced onions and stir for a minute. Add the spinach and fresh fenugreek leaves and stir for 30 seconds or so. Add the tomato wedges and crushed dried fenugreek and stir for another minute or two. Finish with the lime juice. Serve with Naan Bread (see page 192) or Layered Parathas (see page 196).

Cook's note
If you don't have a large enough flat griddle for this dish, you could use a Chinese wok. Just take care not to add too much to it all at once, as this will bring down the temperature, causing all the juices to be released. This would make the dish very wet, which is not the point of this style of cooking!

POTATOES FILLED WITH PANEER AND DRIED FRUIT

This would work very well as a starter; just cut the potato shells in half and serve sprinkled with some chat masala and lemon juice. Served in slightly bigger portions, as below, it makes an impressive main dish for vegetarians. You could really substitute pretty much anything you like for the filling.

SERVES 4

8 medium Desiree potatoes, peeled
2 litres (8 cups) water
2 teaspoons salt
1 teaspoon ground turmeric
vegetable or corn oil for deep-frying

For the filling
4 dried figs, cut into 5mm ($^1/_4$-inch) dice
1 tablespoon raisins
1$^1/_2$ tablespoons paneer, cut into 5mm ($^1/_4$-inch) dice
$^1/_2$ tablespoon cashew nuts, fried in a little oil until golden, then lightly crushed
1 poppadom, fried in oil until crisp, then lightly crushed
2.5cm (1-inch) piece of fresh ginger, finely chopped
2 green chillies, finely chopped
1 tablespoon chopped fresh coriander
$^1/_2$ teaspoon salt
juice of $^1/_2$ lime

For the sauce
400g (14oz) tomatoes, cut in half
1cm ($^1/_2$-inch) piece of fresh ginger, crushed
2 garlic cloves, peeled
2 green cardamom pods
2 cloves
1 bay leaf
125ml ($^1/_2$ cup) water

1 teaspoon red chilli powder
25g (2 tablespoons) butter, diced
3 tablespoons single cream
1 teaspoon dried fenugreek leaves, crushed to a powder
1 teaspoon salt
2 teaspoons sugar

For the marinade
2 tablespoons Greek yoghurt
1 tablespoon single cream
1 teaspoon Ginger Paste (see page 202)
1 teaspoon Garlic Paste (see page 202)
$^1/_2$ teaspoon ground turmeric
$^1/_2$ teaspoon garam masala
$^1/_2$ teaspoon salt

Trim the potatoes with a sharp knife until they are an even cylindrical shape. Now scoop out the inside using a pointed peeler or knife to leave a shell about 5mm ($^1/_4$-inch) thick that is open at one end. Cut the trimmings into 5mm ($^1/_4$-inch) dice and set aside.

Put the water, salt and turmeric in a saucepan and bring to the boil. Add the potatoes and return to the boil, then drain. Dry the potatoes on kitchen paper.

Heat the oil for frying in a deep saucepan or a deep-fat fryer over a low to medium heat, add the potatoes and fry until golden and crisp. Remove and leave to drain on kitchen paper. Now fry the diced potato until golden brown. Drain on kitchen paper.

Mix all the ingredients for the filling with the fried diced potato and carefully use to stuff the potato shells.

For the sauce, put the tomatoes in a large saucepan with the ginger, garlic, cardamom, cloves, bay leaf and water. Bring to the boil and simmer until the tomatoes have completely broken down. Purée in a blender, then strain through a fine sieve into a clean pan. Bring to the boil again, add the chilli powder and simmer until the mixture begins to thicken. Whisk in the butter a little at a time to give a glossy sauce. Add the cream, fenugreek leaves, sugar and salt, mix well, then remove from the heat. Keep warm.

Mix together all the ingredients for the marinade and lightly apply to the outside of the potato shells. Transfer them to a roasting tray, place in an oven preheated to 180°C/350°F/Gas Mark 4 and roast for 10–12 minutes, until the potatoes are heated through and have become slightly coloured and crisp. Remove from the oven and serve with the sauce.

Cook's notes
When frying the potatoes, the trick is to fry them really slowly, so they get cooked properly and do not colour too much.

If you prefer, you could use a slow barbecue to cook the potato shells after filling them.

BOTTLE GOURD AND YELLOW SPLIT PEA CURRY

LAUKI CHANA

This simple dish combining bottle gourd and split peas is popular all over northern India. Some variations finish it with coconut milk, which is just as good.

SERVES 4

200g (1 cup) chana dal (yellow split peas), soaked in cold water for 30 minutes
1 litre (4 cups) water
$1/2$ teaspoon ground turmeric
2.5cm (1-inch) piece of fresh ginger, finely chopped
1 teaspoon salt
3 bottle gourds (lauki or doodhi), peeled, deseeded and cut into 2.5cm (1-inch) dice
2 teaspoons chopped fresh coriander

For tempering
2 tablespoons ghee or vegetable oil
1 teaspoon cumin seeds
2 red chillies
$1/4$ teaspoon asafoetida
1 onion, finely chopped
2 teaspoons ground coriander
1 teaspoon salt
$1/2$ teaspoon garam masala
juice of $1/2$ lemon
$1/2$ teaspoon brown sugar or jaggery
$1/2$ teaspoon coarsely crushed fennel seeds

Drain the split peas and put them in a saucepan with the water, turmeric, ginger and salt. Bring to the boil, skimming off the scum that rises to the surface, then reduce the heat and simmer for 30 minutes or until the split peas are tender but retain a little bite. Add the diced bottle gourds and continue to simmer for 15–20 minutes, until the split peas are very tender and the bottle gourd is cooked through.

For the tempering, heat the ghee or oil in a heavy-based pan, add the cumin seeds and whole red chillies and fry until brown. Add the asafoetida and onion and sauté until the onion is golden brown. Add the ground coriander and salt and cook for 2–3 minutes.

Pour in the cooked split peas and bottle gourd, add the garam masala and simmer over a low heat for about 5 minutes, until the gourd and split peas come together. If you like the dish thick, simply cook it slightly longer until it reaches the desired consistency. Stir in the lemon juice, sugar or jaggery and fennel seeds and garnish with the chopped coriander.

Serve as a vegetarian main course with steamed rice or bread, or as an accompaniment.

SEAFOOD

SPICE-CRUSTED HALIBUT IN GREEN SPICED SAUCE

This is my take on a tandoori fish tikka, traditionally served with green chutney. The only difference is that I use a larger cut of fish and cook it in an ordinary oven rather than a tandoor, while the chutney is transformed into a hot sauce. Served with Lemon Rice (see page 181), it makes a stunning main course.

SERVES 4

4 x 200g (7oz) pieces of halibut fillet
1 tablespoon vegetable or corn oil

For the first marinade
1 teaspoon Ginger Paste (see page 202)
1 teaspoon Garlic Paste (see page 202)
$^1/_2$ teaspoon ground turmeric
1 teaspoon salt

For the second marinade
3 tablespoons Greek-style yoghurt
1 teaspoon yellow chilli powder
$^1/_2$ teaspoon salt
1 teaspoon coriander seeds, roasted in a dry frying pan and then crushed
1 teaspoon fennel seeds, roasted in a dry frying pan and then crushed
$^1/_2$ teaspoon cumin seeds, roasted in a dry frying pan and then crushed
$^1/_2$ teaspoon red chilli flakes

For the sauce
30g (1 cup) mint, roughly chopped
150g (3 cups) fresh coriander, roughly chopped
4 green chillies, finely chopped
250ml (1 cup) water
4 tablespoons vegetable or corn oil
4 garlic cloves, finely chopped
1 onion, finely chopped
5cm (2-inch) piece of fresh ginger, finely chopped
1 tablespoon gram (chickpea) flour
$1^1/_2$ teaspoons salt
1 teaspoon sugar
juice of $^1/_2$ lime

Pat the fish pieces dry on kitchen paper. Mix together all the ingredients for the first marinade, rub them over the fish and set aside for 10 minutes. Heat the oil in a large, non-stick frying pan, add the fish and sear for 1–2 minutes on each side, until lightly golden. Remove from the heat, drain on kitchen paper and keep warm.

Mix all the ingredients for the second marinade together and spread them over the fish. Place on a baking tray and bake in an oven preheated to 220°C/425°F/Gas Mark 7 for 8–10 minutes, turning once, until the fish is cooked through.

Meanwhile, prepare the sauce. Mix the mint, coriander, green chillies, water and half the oil together and blend to a smooth paste in a food processor. Heat the remaining oil in a frying pan, add the garlic, onion and ginger and sauté till golden. Add the gram flour and stir for a few seconds, until the onion turns golden brown, with a sandy texture, and a nice roasted aroma begins to be released. Add the mint and coriander paste, plus the salt and sugar, and cook for about 2–3 minutes without allowing the sauce to discolour. Finish with the lime juice. Serve the fish with the sauce, accompanied by Lemon Rice (see page 181).

Cook's notes
You could apply both the marinades together without searing the fish if you are in a hurry.

To prepare this dish for a dinner party, the fish may be marinated a day before and simply cooked in the oven for 12–14 minutes before serving.

HALIBUT WRAPPED IN BANANA LEAF WITH COCONUT PASTE

This is quite similar to a Thai or Southeast Asian-style fish curry cooked in a banana leaf. Traditionally in India we steam these parcels but they would come out just as well from a low barbecue or an oven. If anything, I prefer them cooked on a barbecue as it adds a smoky element. If you can't get hold of banana leaf, wrap the fish in foil instead.

SERVES 4

4 x 150g (5oz) pieces of halibut fillet, skinned
1 banana leaf, cut into four 30cm (12-inch) squares
$1/2$ teaspoon red chilli flakes

For the coconut paste
1 tablespoon chopped fresh coriander
2 sprigs of mint, chopped
80g (scant 1 cup) fresh coconut, grated
2.5cm (1-inch) piece of fresh ginger, roughly chopped
4 garlic cloves, roughly chopped
6 green chillies, roughly chopped
125ml ($1/2$ cup) thick coconut cream
2 teaspoons cumin seeds, roasted in a dry frying pan
$1/2$ teaspoon ground turmeric
4 tablespoons vegetable or corn oil
juice of 1 lemon
2 teaspoons salt

Put all the ingredients for the coconut paste in a blender or food processor and mix to a smooth paste. Pat the halibut pieces dry and coat them thoroughly with the paste. Set aside for 30 minutes.

Place each piece of fish in a piece of banana leaf, sprinkle with the red chilli flakes and then wrap up the fish in the leaf, taking care to prevent any marinade and juices oozing out during cooking. Place the parcels in a steamer and steam for 10–15 minutes, until the fish is cooked through (or cook them on a low barbecue or in an oven preheated to 200°C/400°F/Gas Mark 6). Open up the parcels a little and serve immediately, with either Green Coconut Chutney (see page 197) or pickled onions.

Cook's note
This is an ideal dish for a dinner party, as you can simply wrap the fish beforehand and cook the parcels 15 minutes before you are ready to serve.

FRESHWATER FISH COOKED WITH ONIONS

BHEKTI DOPYAZA

This is a hugely popular traditional curry from West Bengal. The term *dopyaza* refers to the use of onions at 2 different stages of cooking. Traditionally bhekti fish would be used but tilapia and barramundi also work well.

SERVES 4

800g (1³/₄lb) tilapia, barramundi or similar fish fillets, skinned and cut into 5cm (2-inch) pieces
3 teaspoons salt
2 teaspoons ground turmeric
2 large onions
4 green chillies, deseeded and slit lengthwise in half
2 tablespoons chopped garlic
5cm (2-inch) piece of fresh ginger, finely grated
4 tablespoons ghee
3 tablespoons vegetable or corn oil
3 ripe tomatoes, skinned and chopped
250ml (1 cup) water
3 tablespoons chopped fresh coriander

For the ground spices
1 tablespoon coriander seeds
1 tablespoon cumin seeds
2.5cm (1-inch) piece of cinnamon stick
1 teaspoon green cardamom pods
5 cloves

Wash the fish and pat dry on kitchen paper. Mix with 1 teaspoon of the salt and 1 teaspoon of the turmeric and set aside.

Grind all the spices together using a spice grinder or coffee grinder, or a mortar and pestle.

Slice 1 onion into thick rounds and set aside. Finely chop the remaining onion and mix with the green chillies, garlic and ginger. Finally mix in the ground spices.

Heat the ghee and oil in a large saucepan, add the sliced onion and cook, stirring frequently, until light golden. Remove the onion from the pan with a slotted spoon, allowing the oil to drain back into the pan. Add the finely chopped onion mixture, the remaining turmeric and a teaspoon of the remaining salt to the pan and cook, stirring, for 15–18 minutes, until the colour darkens and the oil begins to separate from the mixture. Stir in the tomatoes and cook until the liquid from the tomatoes has almost evaporated. Add the fish pieces and stir carefully to avoid breaking them up. Add the water and remaining salt, then cover and cook for 12–15 minutes, until the fish is just done. Add the reserved fried onion, then cover and simmer for 3 minutes. Garnish with the chopped coriander and serve with steamed rice.

SEARED SEA BASS FILLET WITH FENUGREEK SAUCE AND POTATO AND BEAN STIR-FRY

This is one of those combinations that turn conventional wisdom about Indian food and wine pairings on its head. I find the herbaceous quality of fenugreek works very well with the Sauvignon Blancs of the New World, while their fresh, clean, mineral aspect is complemented by the mineral quality of the green beans. Try this for yourself!

SERVES 4

4 x 180g (6oz) sea bass fillets, scaled, trimmed and pin-boned
2 tablespoons vegetable or corn oil

For the fenugreek sauce
3 tablespoons vegetable or corn oil
1 onion, finely chopped
1/2 teaspoon ground turmeric
2.5cm (1-inch) piece of fresh ginger, finely chopped
2 green chillies, finely chopped
200g (scant 1 cup) Boiled Cashew Paste (see page 202)
200g (scant 1 cup) plain yoghurt
125ml (1/2 cup) fish stock
1 teaspoon salt
1/2 teaspoon sugar
juice of 1/2 lemon
2 tablespoons dried fenugreek leaves

For the marinade
1 teaspoon salt
1/2 teaspoon cumin seeds, crushed
1/2 teaspoon carom seeds
1 teaspoon finely chopped fresh ginger
juice of 1 lemon

For the potato and bean stir-fry
1 tablespoon vegetable or corn oil
1/2 teaspoon cumin seeds
1 large potato, peeled and cut into 5mm (1/4-inch) dice
1/2 teaspoon salt
a pinch of ground turmeric
75g (3oz) fine green beans, cut into 5mm (1/4-inch) dice

First make the fenugreek sauce. Heat the oil in a heavy-based pan, add the onion and sauté till golden brown. Add the turmeric, ginger and chillies, then stir in the cashew paste. Cook over a low heat, stirring constantly, for 4–5 minutes. Gradually add the yoghurt, stirring to prevent it splitting, then cook over a moderate heat for 2 minutes. Add the fish stock and cook for another 3 minutes. Now add the salt and sugar and adjust the seasoning if necessary. Stir in the lemon juice and fenugreek leaves, then remove from the heat and keep warm.

Pat the fish fillets dry on kitchen paper. Mix together all the ingredients for the marinade, rub them over the fish and set aside for 10 minutes.

Meanwhile, cook the stir-fry. Heat the oil in a large, heavy-based frying pan, add the cumin seeds and let them crackle. Add the potato, salt and turmeric and sprinkle with 1 tablespoon of water. Cover the pan and allow the potato to steam for 3–4 minutes. Remove the lid,

stir the potatoes and add the beans. Cook, uncovered, for another 4–5 minutes, until the potatoes are tender but the beans do not discolour. Remove from the heat and keep warm.

To cook the sea bass, heat the oil in a large, non-stick frying pan, add the fish fillets, skin-side down, and cook over a medium heat for about 2 minutes on each side.

Divide the potato stir-fry between 4 plates and pour the sauce around it, then put the fish on top. Serve with steamed rice.

Cook's note
In order to get a crisp skin, don't move the fish around too much in the pan while it is cooking. You will see the belly side turning slightly opaque and that's a sign that the skin is nice and crisp. Simply turn the fillet over and then take the pan off the heat. The heat retained in the pan will complete the cooking perfectly.

'THIS RATHER SIMPLE DISH, MADE WITH
ROLLED-UP SPICED OMELETTE,
IS QUICK AND EASY, YET IMPRESSIVE.
YOU CAN BE REALLY IMAGINATIVE WITH THE
FLAVOURINGS AND TRY WHATEVER IS IN SEASON.'

OMELETTE CURRY, PAGE 34

BARRAMUNDI WITH KERALA CURRY SAUCE

We use barramundi at The Cinnamon Club but in Kerala, where this dish originates, they use pearl spot, a local fish with a similar texture. If you prefer, you could try sea bass or black bream.

Traditionally this is made with fish and seafood cut into small pieces and simmered in the sauce. I prefer to cook whole fillets separately, as it enables you to appreciate the flavour and texture much better. It also makes for a more attractive presentation, particularly if you leave the skin on.

SERVES 4

4 x 200g (7oz) pieces of barramundi fillet
1 teaspoon salt
$\frac{1}{2}$ teaspoon black onion seeds
$\frac{1}{2}$ teaspoon red chilli flakes
1 tablespoon vegetable or corn oil
2 tablespoons pressed rice flakes (pawa),
   lightly roasted in a dry frying pan
   until golden

For the curry sauce
3 tablespoons vegetable or corn oil
1 teaspoon mustard seeds
$\frac{1}{2}$ teaspoon fenugreek seeds
10 fresh curry leaves
1 large onion, finely chopped
$\frac{1}{2}$ teaspoon ground turmeric
1 teaspoon ground coriander
$1\frac{1}{2}$ teaspoons red chilli powder
3 tomatoes, finely chopped
2 kokum berries (or 2 tablespoons
   tamarind paste)
100ml (scant $\frac{1}{2}$ cup) fish stock
125ml ($\frac{1}{2}$ cup) coconut milk
1 teaspoon salt
juice of $\frac{1}{2}$ lemon

Pat the fish dry with kitchen paper, sprinkle with the salt, black onion seeds and red chilli flakes, then set aside for 30 minutes.

Meanwhile, make the sauce. Heat the oil in a heavy-based pan, add the mustard and fenugreek seeds and let them crackle for 30 seconds. Now add the curry leaves and onion and sauté for 6–8 minutes, until the onion is golden brown. Stir in the ground spices and tomatoes and cook over a high heat until the tomatoes are soft and completely disintegrated. Add the kokum berries and fish stock and simmer for 2–3 minutes. Stir in the coconut milk and salt and simmer for another couple of minutes or until the sauce has a creamy consistency. Squeeze in the lemon juice.

To cook the fish, heat the oil in a large, non-stick frying pan, add the fish fillets, skin-side down, and fry over a medium heat for 2–3 minutes on each side, until cooked through. Sprinkle the rice flakes evenly on top of the fish to form a crust. Pour the sauce on to 4 serving plates, place the fish on top and serve.

BENGALI-STYLE FISH CURRY WITH MUSTARD PASTE

SHORSHE BATA MAACH

This is a classic Bengali curry made using a fresh mustard-seed paste. Traditionally a freshwater fish called rohu is preferred here. It's ever so slightly oily and rich, which gives a unique taste to the dish, but it can be made just as well with any meaty white fish, such as perch, monkfish, cod or halibut.

SERVES 4

800g (1³/₄lb) meaty white fish fillets, skinned and cut into 4cm (1¹/₂-inch) dice
3 tablespoons mustard oil or vegetable oil
1 teaspoon black onion seeds
1 red onion, thinly sliced
2 green chillies, slit lengthwise into quarters
1 teaspoon salt
250ml (1 cup) water
4 tablespoons chopped fresh coriander

For the paste
1 tablespoon black mustard seeds
2 tablespoons yellow mustard seeds
6 green chillies, chopped

For the marinade
1 teaspoon salt
1 tablespoon Garlic Paste (see page 202)
1 tablespoon Ginger Paste (see page 202)
1 tablespoon mustard oil or vegetable oil
1 teaspoon ground turmeric

First make the paste. Put the black and yellow mustard seeds in a small bowl, add just enough water to cover and leave to soak for 3–4 hours. Put the mustard seeds in a small food processor with the green chillies and blitz to a paste, adding a little water. Set aside.

Pat the fish dry on kitchen paper. Mix together all the ingredients for the marinade, add the fish and coat well. Set aside for 10 minutes.

Heat 2 tablespoons of the mustard or vegetable oil in a heavy-based frying pan, add the fish and fry for 3–5 minutes, until just cooked. Remove the fish from the pan and set aside. Heat the remaining oil in the same pan, add the black onion seeds and let them crackle for 30 seconds. Add the red onion and stir for 2–3 minutes, until soft, then add the mustard paste, along with the slit green chillies. Fry the paste for 3–5 minutes, then add the salt, followed by the water. Bring to the boil, reduce the heat and add the fish pieces. Simmer for 2 minutes, then check the seasoning and stir in the chopped coriander. Cover with a lid, remove from the heat and leave to stand for 5–6 minutes. Serve with steamed rice.

Cook's notes
Take care not to make the mustard paste too fine or it will lose its grainy texture. Don't cook it for too long, as it can turn bitter.

Instead of making your own mustard paste, you could use 2 tablespoons of English mustard and 1 tablespoon of wholegrain Dijon mustard.

RAJASTHANI SPICE-CRUSTED MACKEREL WITH YOGHURT KADHI AND SPINACH PORIAL

This is not exactly the sort of dish Mum would cook! Mackerel is not to be found for hundreds of miles from Rajasthan but I find the play of spices with this fish very intriguing. A mixture of cloves, pepper, fennel and cinnamon – all in all quite strong, robust flavours – is more usually associated with the traditional game cooking of Rajasthan. Interestingly, British mackerel stands up really well to the spices and works like a dream.

SERVES 4

1 teaspoon cloves
1 teaspoon fennel seeds
1/2 teaspoon black peppercorns
5cm (2-inch) piece of cinnamon stick
1 teaspoon cumin seeds
1/2 teaspoon red chilli powder
4 large mackerel fillets, pin-boned and trimmed
1 tablespoon vegetable or corn oil
1 teaspoon salt
juice of 1/2 lemon

For the yoghurt kadhi
175g (3/4 cup) plain yoghurt
1 tablespoon gram (chickpea) flour
250ml (1 cup) water
1/2 teaspoon salt
a small pinch of ground turmeric
1 tablespoon ghee
1 dried red chilli
1/2 teaspoon cumin seeds
a sprig of fresh curry leaves
juice of 1/2 lemon

For the curry leaf spinach porial
2 tablespoons corn or vegetable oil
1 teaspoon mustard seeds
a sprig of fresh curry leaves
1 onion, finely chopped
1/2 teaspoon salt
1 green chilli, finely chopped
200g (7oz) spinach, including the stalks, finely shredded
100g (1 cup) fresh or frozen grated coconut

Start with the yoghurt kadhi. Whisk together the yoghurt, gram flour, water, salt and turmeric and pass through a fine sieve to get rid of any lumps. Place in a saucepan over a medium heat and bring to the boil, whisking constantly. Reduce the heat and simmer for 5–8 minutes, until the sauce turns glossy and thickens enough to coat the back of a wooden spoon lightly. Skim off any scum or impurities from the surface. In a small pan, heat the ghee to smoking point. Add the red chilli, cumin seeds and curry leaves and leave for a few seconds, until they splutter and crackle. Tip the contents of the pan over the sauce, squeeze in the lemon juice and set aside.

Prepare the fish next. Pound together all the spices to a coarse consistency, then mix them with the chilli powder. Sprinkle them over the mackerel on both sides. Mix together the oil, salt and lemon juice and drizzle them over the fish. Place the fillets under a hot grill, skin-side up, and cook for 8–10 minutes, until they are just done.

Meanwhile, for the porial, heat the oil in a frying pan, add the mustard seeds and curry leaves and cook for 10–15 seconds, until they start to crackle. Add the onion and sweat for about 5 minutes, until translucent. Now add the salt and chilli and stir for a minute. Add the spinach and cook, stirring, for 2–3 minutes. Finally stir in the coconut and heat through, then remove from the heat.

To assemble, pour the yoghurt kadhi into 4 deep bowls or plates and put the mackerel fillets on top. Place the porial over the fish as a garnish and serve immediately.

Cook's note
Using spinach stalks as well as leaves in the porial gives a much better flavour and texture.

ROAST SALMON WITH DILL AND MUSTARD, GREEN PEA RELISH

You could argue that, strictly speaking, this is not a curry, but by playing about with the proportions of a dish you can get many interesting results and that's precisely what we see here! It makes a fantastic light meal on a hot summer's day. The green pea relish has a kick reminiscent of Japanese wasabi.

SERVES 4

4 x 175g (6oz) pieces of wild salmon
 fillet
1 tablespoon vegetable or corn oil
1 quantity of Green Pea Relish
 (see page 188)

For the first marinade
1 teaspoon Ginger Paste (see page 202)
1 teaspoon Garlic Paste (see page 202)
1 teaspoon salt
1 teaspoon finely ground white pepper
1 teaspoon vegetable or corn oil

For the second marinade
2 tablespoons grated processed Cheddar
 cheese
2 tablespoons Greek-style yoghurt
1 tablespoon wholegrain mustard
2 green chillies, finely chopped
1 tablespoon single cream
1 teaspoon finely chopped dill

Pat the fish dry on kitchen paper. Mix together all the ingredients for the first marinade, rub them over the fish and set aside for 15 minutes.

Meanwhile, make the second marinade. Put the cheese in a small bowl and rub it to a paste with your fingers (a teaspoon of flour could be added to help prevent lumps forming). Add the yoghurt and mix to a smooth paste, then add the wholegrain mustard and chillies and finally mix in the cream and dill.

Heat the oil in a large ovenproof frying pan, add the fish and sear for about 1$\frac{1}{2}$ minutes on each side. Remove from the heat and spread the second marinade over the fish. Transfer to an oven preheated to 180°C/350°F/Gas Mark 4 and cook for 10–12 minutes, until the fish is just done. Drizzle with mustard oil and serve with a dollop of the Green Pea Relish, plus a green salad.

Cook's notes
Rather than marinating the fish when needed, you could keep it in the fridge overnight after applying the second marinade and cook it just before serving. Similarly the chutney can be prepared in advance and served either cold or warm, let down with a little water if it becomes too thick.

This recipes also works very well with swordfish.

BENGALI-STYLE FISH COOKED WITH YOGHURT

DOI MAACH

Doi maach literally translates as 'yoghurt fish'. In some communities, there is a myth that fish and milk should not be consumed at the same meal, as it is bad for the digestion, but this recipe from Bengal dispels the myth by combining the two in the same dish! An age-old favourite, it's an almost permanent fixture at Bengali banquets. It's easy to prepare and goes very well with plain rice.

You could use halibut or, if you want to try a freshwater fish, perch or carp.

SERVES 4

1kg (2½lb) firm white fish fillets, skinned and cut into 4cm (1½-inch) pieces
4 tablespoons mustard oil
3 cloves
2 green cardamom pods
2.5cm (1-inch) piece of cinnamon stick
1 teaspoon black peppercorns
1 dried bay leaf
1 teaspoon mustard seeds
2 onions, finely chopped
1 teaspoon salt
4 green chillies, slit open lengthwise
200g (scant 1 cup) plain yoghurt
1 tablespoon chopped fresh coriander

For the marinade
200g (scant 1 cup) plain yoghurt
1 teaspoon red chilli powder
1 teaspoon ground turmeric
1 tablespoon Ginger Paste (see page 202)
1 tablespoon Garlic Paste (see page 202)

Combine all the ingredients for the marinade, add the fish pieces and mix gently until they are well coated. Set aside to marinate for at least 30 minutes.

Heat 3 tablespoons of the mustard oil in a large, heavy-based pan over a medium heat. Add the cloves, cardamom, cinnamon, peppercorns and bay leaf and fry for 30 seconds, then add the mustard seeds and let them splutter. Add the onions and fry for 4–6 minutes, until translucent. Now add the fish and its marinade and mix gently but thoroughly. Add the salt and cook for 4 minutes, stirring occasionally. Add the slit green chillies, stir in the yoghurt and cook over a medium heat for 6–8 minutes, until the fish is done.

Garnish with the coriander and drizzle the remaining mustard oil over the top. Serve with steamed rice.

ROAST COD FILLET WITH BENGALI-STYLE MUSTARD SAUCE AND RED ONIONS

This is a deconstructed version of a *dopyaza* – a traditional Indian dish that derives its name from the addition of onions at two stages. In my version, the garnish of seared onions adds crunch and visual drama.

SERVES 4

4 x 180g (6oz) pieces of thick cod fillet
   (or pollack or any other firm white fish)
1 tablespoon vegetable or corn oil

For the mustard sauce
2 tablespoons mustard oil
1 bay leaf
$1/2$ teaspoon black onion seeds
$1/2$ teaspoon fennel seeds
1 onion, finely sliced
1 teaspoon Ginger Paste (see page 202)
1 teaspoon Garlic Paste (see page 202)
$1/2$ teaspoon red chilli powder
$1/2$ teaspoon ground turmeric
1 tomato, finely chopped
2 tablespoons wholegrain mustard
500ml (2 cups) fish stock or water
3 green chillies, slit lengthwise in half
1 teaspoon salt
$1/2$ teaspoon sugar
$1/4$ teaspoon garam masala
1 tablespoon chopped fresh coriander

For the marinade
$1/2$ teaspoon black onion seeds
$1/2$ teaspoon fennel seeds
1 dried red chilli, coarsely crushed
1 tablespoon vegetable or corn oil
1 teaspoon salt

To garnish
2 teaspoons ghee or butter
1 red onion, cut into rings
a pinch of black onion seeds
a pinch of salt
juice of $1/2$ lemon

First make the sauce. Heat the oil in a heavy-based pan, add the bay leaf, onion seeds and fennel seeds, then quickly add the onion. Sauté until the onion is golden brown, then add the ginger and garlic pastes, chilli powder and turmeric. Stir-fry over a medium heat for 3–4 minutes, then add the tomato and cook for 4–5 minutes, stirring frequently so the mixture doesn't stick to the bottom of the pan. Add the mustard and cook over a medium heat for 3 minutes. Now pour in the stock or water and bring to a simmer.

Add the green chillies, salt, sugar, garam masala and coriander, then cover the pan and simmer for 2–3 minutes. Check the seasoning, remove from the heat and set aside.

Mix together all the ingredients for the marinade, rub them over the fish and set aside for 10–15 minutes. To cook the fish, heat the oil in a large, ovenproof frying pan, add the cod, skin-side down, and sear for 3 minutes. Turn and sear the other side for 2 minutes, then transfer the pan to an oven preheated to 200°C/ 400°F/Gas Mark 6 for 6–8 minutes, until the fish is just cooked.

Meanwhile, for the garnish, heat the ghee or butter in a frying pan, add the onion rings and cook, stirring constantly, until tender and well browned. Sprinkle with the black onion seeds and salt and drizzle with the lemon juice.

To serve, pour the sauce on to 4 deep plates, place the fish on top and garnish with the onion rings.

POMFRET RECHEADO

This Goan recipe is hardly a curry, in the sense that there is little or no sauce, but the spicing is very upfront and, cooked fresh, the fish doesn't really need a sauce. Although some people cook the fish entirely in a pan, you could finish it in the oven if you prefer. It also works well on a barbecue, as long as it's not too hot.

4 whole pomfret, cleaned
1 teaspoon salt
4 tablespoons vegetable or corn oil
juice of 1 lime

For the spice paste
5cm (2-inch) piece of cinnamon stick
8 green cardamom pods
1 tablespoon cloves
10 dried red chillies
2 tablespoons black peppercorns
2 teaspoons cumin seeds
2 tablespoons groundnut or vegetable
  oil
2 red onions, sliced
12 garlic cloves, chopped
5cm (2-inch) piece of fresh ginger, cut
  into fine strips
250ml (1 cup) dark malt vinegar
2 teaspoons salt
$\frac{1}{2}$ teaspoon sugar

To make the spice paste, roast all the whole spices together in a frying pan over a medium heat for a minute or so, then set aside.
Heat the oil in a frying pan, add the onions, garlic and ginger and sauté until golden brown. Remove from the heat and add to the whole spices. Add the vinegar and leave to soak for about 3 hours (or overnight). Grind the mixture to a coarse paste in a food processor and mix in the salt and sugar.

Slash the fish 2 or 3 times on each side, using a sharp knife. Season with the salt and set aside for 10 minutes. Rub the spice paste over the fish and stuff any excess inside the belly. Set aside for another 30 minutes.

Heat the oil in a large frying pan, add the pomfret and sear for a minute on each side. Transfer to a roasting tray and place in an oven preheated to 180°C/350°F/Gas Mark 4. Cook for 10–12 minutes. Remove from the oven, squeeze the lime juice over and serve with mashed potatoes and/or a green salad.

Cook's note
Feel free to use any white fish for this, such as black bream, sea bass or even Dover sole.

SEARED BLACK BREAM WITH ROASTED AUBERGINE, TOMATO AND POTATO CRUSH AND KACHUMBER

I love this dish for its simplicity. The aubergine crush and kachumber are probably two of the most familiar Indian accompaniments and might be considered mundane in some circumstances, but the combination with a simple fried fillet of bream is stunning. It's a great dish for entertaining, as much of it can be prepared in advance.

SERVES 4

4 black bream fillets (or any white fish), pin-boned
1 tablespoon vegetable or corn oil
1 quantity of Roasted Aubergine, Tomato and Potato Crush (see page 186)

For the kachumber
$1/4$ small cucumber, deseeded and cut into 3mm ($1/8$-inch) dice
$1/2$ carrot, cut into 3mm ($1/8$-inch) dice
1 tomato, deseeded and cut into 3mm ($1/8$-inch) dice
$1/2$ teaspoon salt
1 teaspoon sugar
juice of 1 lemon
2 tablespoons good olive oil
1 tablespoon finely chopped fresh coriander

For the marinade
1 teaspoon salt
$1/2$ teaspoon fennel seeds
$1/2$ teaspoon black onion seeds
$1/2$ teaspoon red chilli flakes

First make the kachumber. Place the diced cucumber, carrot and tomato in a mixing bowl. Whisk together the salt, sugar, lemon juice, olive oil and coriander to make a dressing and mix it with the diced vegetables. Check the seasoning.

Mix together all the ingredients for the marinade, rub them over the fish and set aside for 10 minutes.

Heat the oil in a large, non-stick frying pan, add the black bream fillets, skin-side down, and sear for 3–4 minutes, until well coloured underneath. Turn and cook for another 2 minutes or until just cooked through.

To serve, place the Roasted Aubergine, Tomato and Potato Crush in the centre of each plate and put the fish on top, then drizzle the kachumber around the plate.

TREASURE-OF-THE-EARTH WHOLE FISH COOKED IN A SEALED POT

ZAMEEN DOZ

This dish would originally have been cooked in an earthenware pot, using catfish or freshwater fish such as carp. Local potters would make beautiful fish-shaped pots in different sizes that would be just right for the fish being cooked. A pit would be dug in the ground, then the pot lowered into it, covered with burning cow-dung cakes and left to cook for hours. You can get more or less the same result by cooking the fish in a covered casserole in a very low oven.

Kingfish, pomfret, tilapia, sea bass, small barramundi, trout and black bream would all work well here.

SERVES 4

2 x 900g (2lb) whole fish, cleaned
1 teaspoon salt
juice of 2 limes
2 tablespoons ghee or clarified butter
2 tablespoons chopped coriander stalks
2 tablespoons Crisp Fried Onions
   (see page 203)

For the spice paste
2 blades of mace
6 black peppercorns
seeds from 4 black cardamom pods
   (discard the shells)
3 tablespoons fennel seeds
$1/2$ tablespoon royal (black) cumin seeds
1 tablespoon poppy seeds
1 tablespoon ground almonds
2 tablespoons desiccated coconut
300g ($1^1/4$ cups) Greek-style yoghurt
5cm (2-inch) piece of fresh ginger,
   roughly chopped
5 garlic cloves, roughly chopped
6 cloves, fried in 1 tablespoon ghee

2 teaspoons red chilli powder
4 green chillies, finely chopped
1 teaspoon ground turmeric
3 tablespoons gram (chickpea) flour
a pinch of saffron strands, infused
   in 2 tablespoons warm milk
$1^1/2$ teaspoons salt
$1/2$ teaspoon sugar

To seal
250g ($1^2/3$ cups) plain flour
125ml ($1/2$ cup) water

Slash the fish 3 or 4 times on each side with a sharp knife. Rub in the salt and lime juice and set aside for 15 minutes.

To make the spice paste, lightly roast all the dried whole spices (except the cloves) with the nuts in a dry frying pan, then blitz them to a smooth paste in a food processor with the yoghurt, ginger and garlic. Mix with all the remaining ingredients for the spice paste and smear the fish with the mixture inside and out. Set aside any excess.

Take an earthenware dish, with a tight-fitting lid, that is long enough to hold both fish side by side and grease it with the ghee or clarified butter (alternatively, you could line the dish with a banana leaf). Place the fish in it and cover with any excess spice paste. Mix together the flour and water to make a dough for sealing the lid and stretch it into a thin strip, long enough to cover the edge of the lid all the way round. Stick the dough on to the edge of the lid and place it on the dish, pressing lightly to make sure that it is completely sealed. Place in an oven preheated to 140°C/275°F/ Gas Mark 1 and bake for 1 hour.

Remove the dish from the oven and carefully take the lid off. Sprinkle the chopped coriander stalks and fried onions on top of the fish and serve from the dish.

Cook's note
With a dish like this, don't worry about overcooking the fish. It's quite acceptable to cook it until the flesh is melting off the bone and has thoroughly absorbed the myriad flavours from the spices.

You could ask your fishmonger to butterfly the fish if you prefer to cook it without the bones.

STIR-FRIED SQUID WITH SWEET SPICES AND GREEN MOONG KEDGEREE

Kedgeree, or khichri as it is known in India, is a humble dish perfectly suited to cold, rainy days. When it is combined with smoky-sweet, spicy squid, there is a fascinating interaction of textures and flavours. You can replace the squid with octopus, prawns, shrimps or pretty much any shellfish you like.

SERVES 4

2 tablespoons vegetable or corn oil
500g (1lb 2oz) cleaned squid, cut into 1cm (1/2-inch) rings
50g (1 cup) fresh coriander, chopped
juice of 1 lemon

For the spice paste
10 cloves
1/2 teaspoon black peppercorns
1/2 teaspoon coriander seeds
1/2 teaspoon cumin seeds
2.5cm (1-inch) piece of cinnamon stick
1 tablespoon vegetable or corn oil
1 small onion, finely chopped
2 garlic cloves, finely chopped
1 1/2 teaspoons red chilli powder
1 tablespoon tomato purée
2 dried apricots, finely chopped
1 teaspoon salt
1/2 teaspoon sugar
100ml (scant 1/2 cup) water

For the kedgeree
100g (1/2 cup) split yellow moong lentils
400ml (1 2/3 cups) water
a pinch of ground turmeric
3 tablespoons ghee or clarified butter
1/2 teaspoon cumin seeds
4 garlic cloves, finely chopped
1 large onion, chopped
1cm (1/2-inch) piece of fresh ginger, finely chopped
2 green chillies, finely chopped
1 1/2 teaspoons salt
75g (1/3 cup) basmati rice, boiled
2 tablespoons sprouted green moong lentils
1 tomato, deseeded and cut into 1cm (1/2-inch) dice
2 tablespoons chopped fresh coriander
juice of 1 lemon

For the spice paste, roast the cloves, peppercorns, coriander seeds, cumin seeds and cinnamon stick on a baking sheet in a very low oven for a few minutes to remove any moisture. Grind them to a powder in a spice mill.

Heat the oil in a small pan, add the onion and sauté until golden brown. Add the garlic and sauté for a couple of minutes, then stir in the ground spices and chilli powder. Stir briskly for a few seconds, then add the tomato purée, dried apricots, salt and sugar. Add the water and cook over a medium heat for 4–6 minutes, until the mixture takes on a jammy consistency. Remove from the heat and set aside.

To make the kedgeree, wash the yellow moong lentils, put them in a pan with the water and turmeric and bring to the boil. Simmer for about 20 minutes, until the lentils are tender and all the water has evaporated. Remove from the heat and set aside.

Heat 2 tablespoons of the ghee or butter in a pan, add the cumin seeds and garlic and cook gently until golden. Add the onion and sauté until it begins to colour, then stir in the ginger and green chillies and cook for a minute. Stir in the yellow moong lentils and salt, then fold in the cooked rice. Add the sprouted green moong lentils, tomato and fresh coriander and stir over a low heat for 3–4 minutes. Finish with the remaining tablespoon of ghee or butter and the lemon juice. Remove from the heat and keep warm.

To cook the squid, heat the oil in a large, heavy-based frying pan until it starts to smoke. Add the squid rings and stir quickly until they begin to sear and colour in parts. Add the spice paste and stir-fry for a few seconds, until it coats the squid evenly. Sprinkle in the fresh coriander and squeeze over the lemon juice.

Divide the kedgeree between 4 plates and serve with the squid on top.

Cook's note
The secret to beautifully cooked, juicy squid is getting the pan very hot – i.e. to smoking point – then adding just enough squid to cover the pan in a single layer. If you add too much at once, or put it in an only moderately hot pan, all the juices will come out and the squid will bubble away to rubber. If you don't have a large enough pan to cook all the squid at once, do it in 2 batches.

SEARED SCALLOPS WITH COCONUT AND GINGER SAUCE

Inspired by the Keralan favourite, *moily* – a fish curry made with coconut milk, curry leaves, green chillies and ginger – this recipe highlights the beauty of simplicity. Probably one of the quickest and easiest dishes in the book, it always turns out a winner.

SERVES 4

1 tablespoon vegetable or corn oil
500g (1lb 2oz) fresh king scallops
1 teaspoon sea salt
1 teaspoon coriander seeds, roasted in a dry frying pan and then crushed
$^{1}/_{2}$ teaspoon cumin seeds, roasted in a dry frying pan and then crushed
$^{1}/_{2}$ teaspoon red chilli flakes

For the sauce
2 tablespoons coconut oil or vegetable oil
10 fresh curry leaves
1 onion, sliced
2.5cm (1-inch) piece of fresh ginger, cut into strips
4 green chillies, slit open lengthwise
$^{1}/_{2}$ teaspoon ground turmeric
500ml (2 cups) coconut milk
1 teaspoon salt

First make the sauce. Heat the oil in a large frying pan, add the curry leaves, onion, ginger and green chillies and cook, stirring, until the onion is soft. Add the turmeric, followed by the coconut milk and salt, and bring to a simmer. Cook for 3–5 minutes, until the sauce begins to turn glossy and thickens enough to coat the back of a spoon lightly.

To cook the scallops, heat the oil in a large, heavy-based frying pan, add the scallops and sear for about 1 minute per side, until golden brown. Sprinkle the salt on top and remove from the pan. Mix together the coriander and cumin seeds and chilli flakes and spread them on top of the scallops to give an even crust. Place them under a hot grill for 30 seconds. Serve with the sauce, and some steamed rice on the side.

Cook's note
Some people take the roe off scallops before cooking, but I like to leave it on; it tastes very good with the sauce. You could serve the scallops on wilted spinach or small rice pancakes, if you prefer.

KERALAN-STYLE MIXED SEAFOOD WITH COCONUT AND VINEGAR SAUCE

SEAFOOD MAPPAS

This recipe comes courtesy of Rakesh Nair, our sous-chef at The Cinnamon Club, who besides being a chef happens to have two Masters degrees – one in Mathematics and the other in Computer Sciences! When he introduced me to this recipe, it immediately stood out from typical southern Indian curries. The use of vinegar really lifts the spices and the fish. Easy to make, this one is a must try.

SERVES 4

200g (7oz) headless raw prawns, peeled and de-veined
200g (7oz) salmon fillet, skinned and cut into 2.5cm (1-inch) dice
200g (7oz) white fish fillet, such as halibut, cod or pollack, skinned and cut into 2.5cm (1-inch) dice
100g (3½oz) cleaned squid, cut into rings
200g (7oz) mussels, scrubbed and de-bearded

For the sauce
3 tablespoons vegetable or corn oil
4 garlic cloves, chopped
2.5cm (1-inch) piece of fresh ginger, cut into thin strips
2 red onions, finely sliced
4 green chillies, slit open lengthwise
2 tablespoons ground coriander
250ml (1 cup) seafood stock (or fish stock)
4 tablespoons toddy (palm) vinegar (replace with malt vinegar if necessary)
1 teaspoon salt
250ml (1 cup) coconut milk (if using canned milk, separate the thick milk from the thin part)
1 teaspoon garam masala

For tempering
1 tablespoon coconut oil or vegetable oil
½ teaspoon mustard seeds
10 fresh curry leaves
2 shallots, finely chopped

First make the sauce. Heat the oil in a pan, add the garlic, ginger and onions and sauté for 6–8 minutes, until the onions are really soft. Add the green chillies and ground coriander and cook, stirring, for a minute. Add the stock, vinegar and salt and simmer for 10 minutes.

Now add the prawns and cook over a medium heat for 2–3 minutes. As the sauce thickens, add about half the thin coconut milk, then add the salmon and white fish. Cover the pan and cook over a low heat for 2–3 minutes. Now add the remaining thin coconut milk, followed by the squid, and stir gently. Allow the liquid to come back to a simmer and then add the mussels. Simmer only until the mussels have opened up, then stir in the garam masala and thick coconut milk and remove from the heat.

To make the tempering, heat the oil in a small frying pan and add the mustard seeds, followed by the curry leaves and shallots. Sauté until the shallots have turned golden. Pour the tempering over the curry and cover with a lid. Leave for 5 minutes, to allow the flavours to permeate, then serve with steamed rice.

PRAWN BALCHAO

Although you could store this in the fridge for several days and serve it hot or cold as a pickle, it tastes just as delicious fresh and hot. You may find the portions slightly small for a main course but it works best combined with other dishes, and on its own may be a bit too spicy and full-on for a balanced meal. Try to combine it with a mild and saucy curry, such as Seafood Mappas (see page 84).

SERVES 4

4 tablespoons vegetable or corn oil
3 red onions, chopped
10 fresh curry leaves
1 tablespoon Ginger Paste (see page 202)
1 tablespoon Garlic Paste (see page 202)
4 green chillies, slit open lengthwise
$^1/_2$ teaspoon ground turmeric
600g (1lb 5oz) medium prawns, peeled
2 teaspoons salt
1 teaspoon sugar
3 tablespoons malt vinegar

For the spice mix
1 tablespoon cumin seeds
1 tablespoon black peppercorns
10 dried red chillies

For the spice mix, roast the ingredients separately in a dry frying pan over a medium heat for a minute or so, then grind together until fine.

Heat the oil in a large frying pan, add the onions and curry leaves and cook, stirring, until golden brown. Add the ginger and garlic pastes and green chillies and stir for a minute. Add the turmeric, followed by the spice mix and prawns, and sauté over a high heat for 4–5 minutes, until the prawns are cooked. Add the salt, sugar and malt vinegar and cook for another 4–5 minutes, until the oil separates from the mixture. Serve with steamed rice.

Cook's note
You could make the mixture as above, but omitting the prawns, then spread it over large butterflied prawns and grill them. Served with a salad of your choice, this makes an excellent summer lunch, washed down with a glass of fruity white wine.

KING PRAWNS COOKED IN SAFFRON KORMA SAUCE

JHINGA NISHA

This recipe from the courts of the Nawabs of Lucknow is a fine example of sophisticated Muslim cooking. Rich and regal, it is a true celebration dish. It may well have been the original korma that has been severely travestied many times over to end up in the ubiquitous British high-street curry house.

SERVES 4

1kg (2¼lb) king prawns, peeled and de-veined (keep 200g (7oz) of the shells for the stock)
6 green cardamom pods
3 blades of mace
60g (⅔ cup) blanched almonds
60g (⅔ cup) unsalted cashew nuts
3 tablespoons ghee
2 large onions, finely chopped
4 green chillies, finely chopped
5cm (2-inch) piece of fresh ginger, finely chopped
a pinch of saffron strands, infused in 3 tablespoons warm milk
1½ teaspoons salt
100ml (scant ½ cup) single cream
2 tablespoons finely chopped fresh coriander

For the stock
500ml (2 cups) water
¼ teaspoon ground turmeric
2 green cardamom pods
2 blades of mace
1 bay leaf
½ carrot, thickly sliced
2 garlic cloves, crushed
2 black peppercorns

First make the stock. Wash the 200g reserved prawn shells in cold water and place them in a large pan with all the remaining stock ingredients. Bring to the boil, then reduce the heat and simmer for 15 minutes. Strain through a fine sieve and set aside.

Grind 3 of the cardamom pods and 1 blade of mace in a mortar and pestle, then set aside.

Add the almonds and cashew nuts to a pan of boiling water and simmer for 30–40 minutes, until softened. Drain well, reserving the liquid. Place the nuts in a food processor and blitz to a smooth paste, adding some of the reserved cooking liquid if required.

Heat the ghee in a wide, shallow pan over a medium heat. Add the remaining cardamom pods and mace blades and stir for 30 seconds. Now add the onions and sauté until golden. Add the chillies and ginger and sauté for 1 minute, then mix in the nut paste. Stir over a low to medium heat for 6–8 minutes, until the ghee separates out and the paste starts to leave the side of the pan.

Add the prawns and 4 tablespoons of the stock. Keep stirring, adding a further 2–4 tablespoons of stock 2 or 3 times, until the prawns begin to turn pink and the sauce is a coating consistency. Mix in the saffron milk and salt and simmer for a minute longer, until the prawns are cooked. Add the cream, heat through and transfer to a serving dish. Sprinkle with the ground mace and cardamom and the fresh coriander. Serve with steamed basmati rice or Layered Parathas (see page 196).

Cook's note
Take care while simmering the almond and cashew paste, as it may splutter and cause a nasty injury. The safest way is to cook it with the lid on, removing the lid every minute or so to stir with a long-handled spatula.

WILD PRAWNS BAKED WITH COCONUT AND MUSTARD

BHAPA BAGDA

This would make a great party dish, and it's certainly one that will impress. In India it is reserved for special occasions and intimate gatherings. The use of coconut, mustard, chilli and ginger creates an interesting play of flavours; the sweetness of the prawns and coconut is balanced by the heat from the chilli and ginger and the pungency of the mustard oil.

SERVES 4

8 large wild prawns (or ordinary large prawns if you can't get wild ones)
250ml (1 cup) thick coconut milk
100ml (scant ½ cup) Greek yoghurt
75g (3 oz) yellow mustard seeds, soaked overnight in just enough water to cover, then blended to a paste with 2 tablespoons white vinegar
6 green chillies, slit open lengthwise
5cm (2-inch) piece of fresh ginger, cut into thin strips
2 teaspoons salt
1½ teaspoons sugar
2 tablespoons Ginger-Garlic Paste (see page 202)
5 tablespoons mustard oil
1 teaspoon black mustard seeds
50g (1 cup) fresh coriander, finely chopped
1 teaspoon garam masala

Slice each prawn horizontally in half, with the head and shell still on. With the point of a sharp knife, remove the dark intestinal vein that runs down the back, then pat the prawns dry on kitchen paper.

Whisk together the coconut milk, yoghurt, mustard seed paste, chillies, ginger, salt, sugar, and ginger-garlic paste, then set aside.

In a frying pan, heat the mustard oil to smoking point and then let it cool. Reheat the oil and add the mustard seeds. Once they crackle, add the coconut and spice mixture and bring to the boil over a low heat, whisking constantly; be careful not to let the mixture separate. Simmer gently for 2–3 minutes, then remove from the heat.

Arrange the slit prawns on a baking tray, shell-side down. Pour the sauce over the tails and cover the tray with foil. Place in an oven preheated to 180°C/350°F/Gas Mark 4 and cook for 15–18 minutes, until the prawns are done. Remove from the oven, sprinkle with the chopped coriander and garam masala and serve immediately, with steamed rice.

Cook's note
You could simmer the prawns in a large, wide casserole dish instead of baking them; just take care not to move them around too much or they will break. They will still taste great, however!

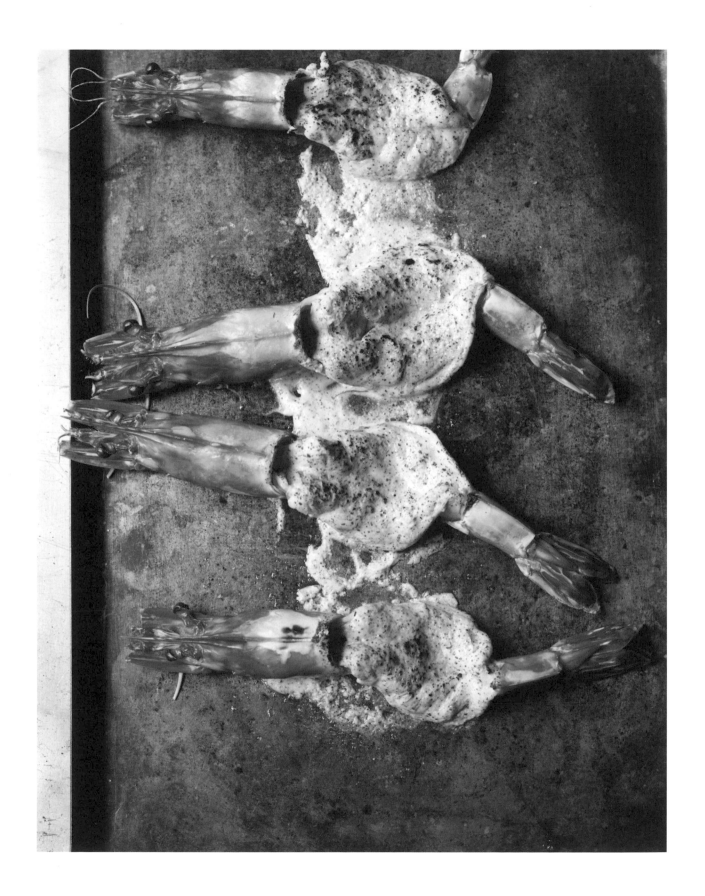

PRAWNS IN KERALA CURRY

This is one of my favourite curries. I still remember an outstanding version cooked for me on a boat in the backwaters of Kerala. It's hard to imagine something as simple as this could taste so delicious.

This is the complete opposite of what people tend to expect from Indian curries. Rather than being rich, heavy and thick, it has fresh flavours and a lightness of touch that quite simply make it one of the best curries of all time.

4 tablespoons vegetable or corn oil
$^1/_2$ teaspoon black peppercorns
1 teaspoon mustard seeds
$^1/_2$ teaspoon fenugreek seeds
10 fresh curry leaves
2 red onions, chopped
$^1/_2$ teaspoon ground turmeric
1 teaspoon ground coriander
2 teaspoons mild red chilli powder
2 tomatoes, finely chopped
1 teaspoon salt
20 king prawns, peeled and de-veined
4 kokum berries (or 2 tablespoons tamarind paste)
150ml ($^2/_3$ cup) seafood stock (or fish stock)
200ml (scant 1 cup) coconut milk

Heat the oil in a pan, add the peppercorns, mustard and fenugreek seeds, followed by the curry leaves and onions, and sauté until golden brown. Add the ground spices, tomatoes and salt and cook until the tomatoes are soft and completely disintegrated. Add the prawns and toss well for 3–5 minutes to coat them in the spice mixture. Stir in the kokum berries and stock and simmer for 2–3 minutes. Stir in the coconut milk and simmer for another 3–5 minutes, until the prawns are cooked and the sauce has a creamy consistency. Check the seasoning and adjust if necessary. Serve with steamed rice.

Cook's note

You could make this with a variety of seafood instead of simply prawns. Just be sure to work out a sequence in which to add them to the curry. It's best to start with firm fish, if using any, followed by prawns, then add mussels and squid at the end.

KADHAI LOBSTER

A kadhai is an Indian wok, usually made of iron, that differs from the Chinese wok in that it is much heavier and has 'ears' on the sides. Rather like Chinese stir-fries, Indian kadhai dishes are drier than traditional curries and use quick-cooking ingredients over a high heat, with the addition of crushed spices rather than finely ground ones.

Usually chicken, thin strips of lamb, pre-cooked kebabs or paneer are cooked using this method but I've taken it to another level by using lobster. It's a dish fit for a celebration!

SERVES 4

2 x 675g (1^1/$_2$lb) live lobsters
1 tablespoon butter
1 onion, diced
^{1}/$_2$ red pepper, deseeded and diced
^{1}/$_2$ yellow pepper, deseeded and diced
4 green chillies, slit open and cut into 8 pieces each
1 teaspoon red chilli flakes
^{1}/$_2$ teaspoon freshly cracked black peppercorns
1 tablespoon single cream
1 teaspoon dried fenugreek leaves, crushed with your fingertips
juice of ^{1}/$_2$ lemon
2 tablespoons chopped fresh coriander

For the kadhai masala
4 tablespoons vegetable oil
2 green cardamom pods
2.5cm (1-inch) piece of cinnamon stick
1 teaspoon cumin seeds, coarsely crushed
1 teaspoon coriander seeds, coarsely crushed
1 teaspoon fennel seeds, coarsely crushed

2 red onions, finely chopped
3 garlic cloves, chopped
2.5cm (1-inch) piece of fresh ginger, finely chopped
2 teaspoons red chilli powder
4 tomatoes, deseeded and finely chopped
1^1/$_2$ teaspoons salt
^{1}/$_2$ teaspoon garam masala

Put the lobsters in the freezer for about 2 hours, until comatose. Then plunge them into a large pan of boiling water and simmer for just 3 minutes. Remove from the pan and place them in a large bowl of ice for about 15 minutes, until chilled. Cut each lobster lengthwise in half and remove the flesh from the shell. Twist the claws off the body and crack them using the heel of a heavy knife. Remove the claw meat from the shells and set aside. Cut the body meat into 1cm (^{1}/$_2$-inch) dice and set aside.

For the kadhai masala, heat the oil in a kadhai or heavy-based pan, add the cardamom, cinnamon, cumin, coriander and fennel seeds and let them crackle. Add the chopped onions and sauté until golden brown, then add the garlic, ginger and red chilli powder and sauté for 1–2 minutes. Now add the chopped tomatoes and cook for 4–6 minutes, until the tomatoes are soft and the mix is homogenised. Stir in the salt and garam masala, remove from the heat and set aside.

In a separate pan, heat the butter and sear the lobster claw meat until lightly coloured all over. Add the onion, peppers and green chillies and sauté for about 3 minutes, until softened. Add the diced lobster meat and sauté over a high heat for 2 minutes. Add the chilli flakes and cracked pepper, then pour in the cooked masala and simmer for 2–3 minutes. Once the lobster meat is cooked through, check the seasoning. Stir in the cream and fenugreek, then finish with the lemon juice and chopped coriander. Serve with steamed rice.

Cook's notes
A fantastic way to present this dish is in the lobster shells. Simply dry the shells out first by putting them in a moderate oven for 5–6 minutes.

Although this is a kadhai dish, it works just as well in a tawa – i.e. a flat iron griddle. If using a griddle, just call your dish Tawa Lobster instead!

'…NOT EXACTLY THE SORT OF DISH MUM WOULD COOK! MACKEREL IS NOT TO BE FOUND FOR HUNDREDS OF MILES FROM RAJASTHAN BUT I FIND THE PLAY OF SPICES WITH THIS FISH VERY INTRIGUING.'

RAJASTHANI SPICE-CRUSTED MACKEREL
WITH YOGHURT KADHI AND SPINACH PORIAL, PAGE 66

BENGALI-STYLE GRILLED LOBSTER

This is a very simple curry. The flavours are light and clean but it is the taste of the lobster that is most pronounced – as it should be! It makes an ideal light main course or a starter for an elaborate dinner party.

SERVES 4

2 x 675g (1¹/₂lb) live lobsters
2 tablespoons vegetable or corn oil
1 teaspoon salt
1 teaspoon ground cardamom
¹/₂ teaspoon sugar
2 tablespoons chopped fresh coriander
2 tablespoons thick coconut milk
juice of 1 lemon

For the claw meat
2 tablespoons vegetable or corn oil
1 large onion, finely chopped
2.5cm (1-inch) piece of fresh ginger, finely chopped
¹/₂ teaspoon red chilli powder
1 teaspoon red chilli flakes
1 teaspoon coriander seeds
1 teaspoon fennel seeds
1 tomato, finely chopped
1 teaspoon salt

Put the lobsters in the freezer for about 2 hours, until comatose. Then plunge them into a large pan of boiling water and simmer for just 3 minutes. Remove from the pan and place in a large bowl of ice for about 15 minutes, until chilled. Cut each lobster lengthwise in half. Twist the claws off the body and crack them open using the heel of a heavy knife, then remove the meat and set aside. Pat the lobster halves dry on kitchen paper.

Heat the oil in a large, heavy-based frying pan, add the lobster halves, flesh-side down, and sear for 1 minute, until the meat just starts to colour. Remove the lobsters from the pan and sprinkle with the salt, cardamom, sugar and coriander. Drizzle the coconut milk and lemon juice over and place under a hot grill for 8–10 minutes, until the lobster is cooked through and a light crust has formed.

Meanwhile, cook the claw meat. Heat the oil in a small frying pan, add the onion and sauté until golden brown. Add the claw meat and stir-fry over a high heat for 1–2 minutes. Add the ginger, chilli powder, chilli flakes, coriander and fennel seeds and sauté for a couple of minutes more. Now add the tomato and cook for about 3 minutes, until the tomatoes has blended in well and the mix is coating the claw meat. Season with the salt and remove from the heat.

Pile up the claw meat in the head cavity of the lobster halves and serve with a salad.

MEAT

RACK OF LAMB WITH SAFFRON SAUCE

This is the type of recipe that cries out to be modernised. It was one of the first to get me thinking about deconstructing traditional Indian dishes and creating contemporary versions. I've always maintained that simmering a fine rack of lamb in a sauce until it is cooked through is a waste of good meat. Instead, this method of roasting the meat separately and serving it with a sauce made according to the principles of French cuisine adds a different dimension to the concept of curry.

SERVES 4

2 racks of lamb, cut in half
1 tablespoon vegetable or corn oil

For the marinade
1 tablespoon Ginger Paste (see page 202)
1 tablespoon Garlic Paste (see page 202)
1 teaspoon red chilli powder
1 tablespoon vegetable or corn oil
1 teaspoon salt
juice of 1 lemon
2 tablespoons Greek-style yoghurt
1 tablespoon chopped fresh coriander
$^1/_2$ teaspoon garam masala

For the saffron sauce
1 tablespoon vegetable or corn oil
2 black cardamom pods
4 cloves
1 blade of mace
2 bay leaves
400g (14oz) tomatoes, roughly chopped
1 large onion, roughly chopped
2.5cm (1-inch) piece of fresh ginger, crushed
2 garlic cloves, crushed
2 teaspoons mild red chilli powder

500ml (2 cups) chicken stock or water
1 teaspoon salt
$^1/_2$ teaspoon sugar
$^1/_4$ teaspoon garam masala
a small pinch of saffron strands
2 tablespoons single cream
1 tablespoon cold butter

If the racks haven't already been prepared, trim off the skin and fat, leaving just a thin layer of fat on the meat. Mix together all the ingredients for the marinade. Rub them over the lamb and set aside for 30 minutes.

To make the sauce, heat the oil in a large saucepan, add the whole spices and the bay leaves and let them crackle. Add the tomatoes, onion, ginger, garlic and chilli powder and cook for 4–5 minutes. Add the stock or water and simmer over a low heat for about 15 minutes, until the tomatoes have completely broken down and the onion is very soft. Purée in a blender or food processor, then strain through a fine sieve into a clean pan. Bring back to the boil and simmer until the sauce thickens enough to coat the back of a wooden spoon. Add the salt, sugar and garam masala, then sprinkle in the saffron and simmer for 2–3 minutes. Adjust the seasoning if necessary. Just before serving, stir in the cream and finally finish the sauce by stirring in the cold butter.

To cook the lamb, heat the oil in a large, heavy-based frying pan, then add the lamb racks and sear over a high heat until browned all over. Transfer to a roasting tray and place in an oven preheated to 200°C/400°F/Gas Mark 6. Roast for 10–15 minutes, depending on how well done you like your meat. Remove from the oven and leave to rest in a warm place for 5 minutes.

Divide the sauce between 4 serving plates, place the lamb on top and serve immediately.

Cook's note
The butter and cream emulsify the sauce, so it is best to add them at the very end after checking the seasoning. Don't let the sauce boil after adding the butter or it will separate and become thin.

RAAN

The grandest of Indian dishes, this is curry but not as we know it. It combines two cooking techniques, braising and roasting, and the result is highly impressive.

Although the recipe calls for lamb, feel free to use hogget, mutton or even goat.

SERVES 8–10

2 legs of lamb, weighing about 1.5kg each, trimmed of any surface fat
2 tablespoons red chilli powder
5 tablespoons Ginger Paste (see page 202)
6 tablespoons Garlic Paste (see page 202)
250ml (1 cup) malt vinegar
500g (2 cups) plain yoghurt
3 onions, sliced and fried until crisp (see page 203)
2 teaspoons royal (black) cumin seeds
1 tablespoon salt
6 bay leaves
3 cinnamon sticks, about 5cm (2 inches) each
5 green cardamom pods
2 tablespoons melted butter
2 teaspoons lemon juice
1 teaspoon chat masala
4 tablespoons single cream
1 teaspoon garam masala
1 tablespoon chopped fresh coriander

With the tip of a sharp knife, cut small incisions in the lamb legs at approximately 5cm (2-inch) intervals. Mix together the red chilli powder, ginger paste, garlic paste, vinegar, yoghurt, fried onions, royal cumin and salt, then massage them over the legs, rubbing and pressing the spices into the gashes created by the knife. Set aside for 15 minutes.

Put the legs, drained of all marinading liquid, on an oiled baking tray, add the bay leaves, cinnamon and green cardamom, then cover the tray with foil. Place in an oven preheated to 180°C/350°F/Gas Mark 4 and braise for 2½ hours, until the meat is very tender and ready to fall off the bone. Remove from the oven and leave to cool. Remove the legs from the liquid and allow them to dry. Pass the liquid through a fine sieve and reserve to make the sauce.

Take the meat off the bone and cut it into 5cm (2-inch cubes). Thread them on to 8–10 metal skewers and roast on a barbecue or under a very hot grill, basting frequently with the melted butter, until crisp and well browned. Finish with a drizzle of lemon juice, any leftover melted butter and the chat masala.

For the sauce, bring the cooking juices to the boil in a small pan and simmer until reduced to a coating consistency. Correct the seasoning and stir in the cream, garam masala and fresh coriander. Pour the sauce over the meat and serve with Naan Bread (see page 192).

Cook's note
It's important to drain all the liquid from the legs before roasting them, in order to get a crisp finish.

MODERN RAAN

Traditionally, raan is braised, as in the previous recipe, but I find that if the meat is good quality it can be roasted instead and works just as well, if not better. I've added a step of tunnel-boning the leg (you could ask your butcher to do this) to create a pocket, which can be filled with paneer cheese and dried fruits. This makes it truly special, just as a raan should be! Also, roasting this way keeps the meat moist compared to braising, where the meat is cooked through and therefore can be dry.

SERVES 4

1 leg of young lamb, weighing about
   1.5 kg (3^1/$_4$lb)

For the marinade
250g (1 cup) Greek-style yoghurt
1 tablespoon Ginger Paste (see page 202)
1 tablespoon Garlic Paste (see page 202)
2 tablespoons Fried Onion Paste
   (see page 203)
1 teaspoon red chilli powder
^{1}/$_2$ teaspoon garam masala
1 tablespoon chopped fresh coriander
1^1/$_2$ teaspoons salt
2 tablespoons vegetable or corn oil

For the filling
60g (^{1}/$_2$ cup) khoya (reduced milk cakes,
   available in Indian stores), grated
75g (^{1}/$_2$ cup) paneer, grated
60g (^{1}/$_2$ cup) Cheddar cheese, grated
2 onions, sliced and fried until crisp
   (see page 203)
4 dried figs, cut into 5mm (^{1}/$_4$-inch) dice
4 dried apricots, cut into 5mm (^{1}/$_4$-inch)
   dice
1 tablespoon raisins

2 tablespoons cashew nuts, fried in
   a little oil until golden
5cm (2-inch) piece of fresh ginger,
   chopped
4 green chillies, chopped
^{1}/$_2$ teaspoon royal (black) cumin
   seeds
1 teaspoon salt
juice of 1 lime

For the onion salad
2 red onions, thinly sliced
^{1}/$_2$ cucumber, halved lengthwise and
   thinly sliced
1 carrot, cut into thin strips
1 tomato, deseeded and thinly sliced
^{1}/$_2$ teaspoon salt
^{1}/$_2$ teaspoon cumin seeds, roasted in
   a dry frying pan and then crushed
1 tablespoon chopped fresh
   coriander
juice of ^{1}/$_2$ lime

Trim the excess fat off the lamb and, if your butcher hasn't tunnel-boned it for you, remove the thighbone by cutting around it carefully with a carving knife to leave a cavity. Prick the leg on the outside with a fork.

Combine all the ingredients for the marinade. Rub the marinade over the leg of lamb, both outside and inside the cavity, and leave for 15 minutes.

To make the filling, combine all the ingredients and then use to stuff the lamb leg. Truss the leg using a butcher's needle and twine to close the open part completely. Transfer

to a roasting tray and place in an oven preheated to 220°C/425°F/ Gas Mark 7. Roast for 10 minutes, then reduce the heat to 180°C/ 350°F/Gas Mark 4 and cook for a further 50 minutes. Remove from the oven and leave to rest for about 30 minutes.

Meanwhile, make the onion salad. Put all the cut vegetables except the tomato in a bowl of ice-cold water for 10 minutes to crisp them up. Strain and sprinkle with the salt, cumin and fresh coriander. Squeeze the lime juice over.

Cut the meat into slices 1cm (^{1}/$_2$ inch) thick and serve with the onion salad.

Cook's note
For something like this to be enjoyed at it's best, it is very important to rest the meat before serving. This makes it more tender and you won't lose the juices when you slice it.

SPICED MINCED LAMB WITH LIVER

KEEMA KALEJI

This rustic dish is one of the best examples of Punjabi *dhaba*-style cooking. You find these dishes featured in roadside cafés all over northern India. If you do get the chance to eat in these places, a word of caution: order this dish in a well-known and very busy place only, as it could be dodgy otherwise.

Although this is cooked in a saucepan here, it can be made just as well in a wok (kadhai) or even on a flat griddle (tawa).

SERVES 4

4 tablespoons vegetable oil or ghee
1 bay leaf
2.5cm (1-inch) piece of cinnamon stick
2 green cardamom pods
4 red onions, finely chopped
4 garlic cloves, finely chopped
2.5cm (1-inch) piece of fresh ginger, finely chopped
2 teaspoons red chilli powder
2 green chillies, finely chopped
1 teaspoon red chilli flakes
1 teaspoon ground turmeric
2 teaspoons ground cumin
1^1/$_2$ teaspoons salt
3 tomatoes, blended to a purée
500g (1lb 2oz) lean minced lamb
250g (1 cup) plain yoghurt
250g (9oz) lamb's liver, cut into 2cm (^{3}/$_4$-inch) dice

To finish
^{1}/$_4$ teaspoon garam masala
stalks from ^{1}/$_2$ bunch of coriander, finely chopped
juice of 1 lime or lemon

Heat 3 tablespoons of the oil or ghee in a heavy-based pan, add the bay leaf, cinnamon and cardamom pods and let them crackle. Add the chopped onions and fry over a moderate heat for 6–8 minutes, until they begin to turn golden brown. Add the garlic, ginger, chilli powder, green chillies, chilli flakes, turmeric, cumin and salt and stir-fry for about 6 minutes, until the mixture is cooked and brown. Add the puréed tomatoes and cook for 5 minutes. Raise the heat, add the mince and cook, stirring constantly to prevent lumps, for 5–6 minutes, until well browned all over.

Cover the pan, lower the heat and simmer for 10 minutes. When the moisture has evaporated and the mince is cooked, stir in the yoghurt. Cook for 3–4 minutes, until thoroughly blended.

Heat the remaining oil or ghee in a separate pan, add the diced liver and sear quickly for a minute or so, until browned on the outside. Tip it into the simmering mince. Stir in the garam masala, coriander stalks and lime or lemon juice. Serve hot, with chapattis or Layered Parathas (see page 196).

Cook's notes
If you want to add another texture to the mince, boil 2 eggs for 6–8 minutes, then peel them. Chop the whites and mix them into the mince, then grate the yolks on top as a garnish.

I have tried several variations, using sweetbreads, kidney and even brains instead of liver, and they all work very well.

LAMB NECK FILLET WITH MASALA MASH

Properly marinated lamb middle neck cooked in a slow tandoor is a thing of beauty, as I have found out over the years. Lamb neck is an unbelievably underrated cut. People seem to go crazy over best end of lamb but, besides being expensive, quite often it doesn't match up to the flavour and texture you can get from the neck. Here I roast the fillet with tandoori spicing and serve it with a creamy masala mash and herbaceous sauce.

SERVES 4

4 lamb neck fillets (about 750g
   (1lb 10oz) in total), trimmed
2 tablespoons vegetable or corn oil
Masala Mash (see page 181), to serve

For the marinade
1 tablespoon Ginger-Garlic Paste
   (see page 202)
1 teaspoon salt
$^1/_2$ teaspoon coarsely ground white
   pepper
2 tablespoons Greek-style yoghurt
1 tablespoon single cream
1 tablespoon cream cheese
2.5cm (1-inch) piece of fresh ginger,
   finely chopped
2 green chillies, finely chopped
1 tablespoon chopped fresh coriander
$^1/_2$ teaspoon Mace and Cardamom
   Powder (see page 204)
$^1/_2$ teaspoon salt

For the sauce
2 tablespoons ghee
3 green chillies, roughly chopped
100g (scant $^1/_2$ cup) Boiled Cashew Paste
   (see page 202)

4 tablespoons plain yoghurt
$^1/_2$ teaspoon ground turmeric
250ml (1 cup) lamb stock or water
1 red onion, cut into 1cm ($^1/_2$-inch)
   dice
1 tomato, deseeded and cut into
   1cm ($^1/_2$-inch) dice
1 tablespoon single cream
juice of 1 lemon
1 teaspoon salt
1 tablespoon dried fenugreek leaves
4 tablespoons fresh coriander leaves

Mix all the ingredients for the marinade together, rub them over the lamb and set aside for 30 minutes.

Meanwhile, make the sauce. Heat the ghee in a pan, add the green chillies and cashew paste and cook over a medium heat for 5 minutes. Whisk in the yoghurt and cook for another 3–4 minutes. Stir in the turmeric, then the stock or water and simmer for about 5–6 minutes, until it is thick enough to coat the back of a spoon. Add the onion and tomato and cook for a minute longer. Stir in the cream, lemon juice and salt, sprinkle in the fenugreek and coriander, then remove from the heat and keep warm.

To cook the lamb, remove it from the marinade, reserving the leftover marinade. Heat the oil in a large, ovenproof frying pan, add the neck fillets and sear for about a minute on each side until lightly coloured. Transfer the pan to an oven preheated to 180°C/350°F/Gas Mark 4 and roast for 8 minutes.

Leave the meat to rest for 5 minutes, then spread the leftover marinade over it and flash it under a hot grill for 2 minutes or until it is lightly crisped up. Slice the fillets into 4 pieces each and serve with the sauce and Masala Mash.

Cook's note
You could cook the lamb fillets through completely on a barbecue rather than frying and roasting them.

HYDERABADI-STYLE LAMB BIRYANI

HYDERABADI KACCHI BIRYANI

This style of making biryani will always remain an enigma for anyone who has not seen it done. When I returned from a stint in Hyderabad in my training days and described the way it was made, everyone, including my tutors, thought I was pulling a fast one. No one would believe that you could start with raw meat and cooked rice in a pot and end up with the best biryani in the world. After all, the logical way of cooking this would be by starting with cooked meat and raw rice...but maybe that's why this example of black magic deserves its place in the book!

Before you start, you must make sure you have the right utensils for the job. You will need a heavy pot with a tight-fitting lid, large enough for the meat and rice to fill it by no more than two-thirds. This allows the steam to build up and assist the cooking, as well as helping to make the rice light and fluffy rather than stodgy and dense. At the same time, too large a pot will not work either.

If the pot you have is not the right size, just adjust the quantities and make the biryani in batches if need be. Traditionally it is a one-pot dish and well suited to feeding large numbers.

SERVES 4–6

1kg (2¼lb) boned leg of lamb, cut into 2.5cm (1-inch) dice (you could also use a few pieces on the bone)
5 tablespoons chopped fresh coriander
6 green chillies, slit open lengthwise
2 tablespoons ghee or vegetable oil

1g (about ¼ teaspoon) saffron strands, soaked in 125ml (½ cup) milk
4 tablespoons single cream

For the marinade

2 tablespoons Ginger-Garlic Paste (see page 202)
1 bay leaf
6 green cardamom pods
1 blade of mace
⅛ nutmeg, grated
½ teaspoon cloves
5cm (2-inch) piece of cinnamon stick
1 tablespoon red chilli powder
1 teaspoon ground turmeric
¼ small green papaya, peeled, deseeded and finely grated
500g (2 cups) plain yoghurt
2 teaspoons salt
1 teaspoon sugar
5 large onions, finely sliced and fried until crisp (see page 203)

For the rice

2.5 litres (2½ quarts) water
2 black cardamom pods
4 green cardamom pods
½ teaspoon cloves
75g (3½ cups) mint, chopped
1 tablespoon salt
600g (3 cups) basmati rice, washed and then soaked in cold water for 30 minutes
4 tablespoons ghee

To seal

250g (1 cup) plain flour
125ml (½ cup) water

Mix all the ingredients for the marinade together, setting aside half the fried onions for later use. Mix the lamb with the marinade and set aside for at least 3 hours.

Now cook the rice. Bring the water to the boil in a large pan, then add the whole spices, half the mint and the salt. Simmer for 5 minutes or so. Now add the soaked rice and simmer, uncovered, for 5–6 minutes, until the rice is half cooked. Drain through a colander and set aside. Melt the ghee in a small pan, then set aside.

Take a large, heavy-based casserole with a tight-fitting lid and put the marinated meat in it. Sprinkle with half the chopped coriander, the remaining mint and half the reserved fried onions. Spread the rice over the meat. Sprinkle with the remaining coriander and fried onions, plus the green chillies, melted ghee, saffron milk and cream.

Mix together the flour and water to make a dough for sealing the lid and stretch it into a thin strip, long enough to cover the edge of the lid all the way round. Stick the dough on to the edge of the lid and place it on the casserole, pressing lightly to make sure that it is well sealed. Place the sealed pot over a high heat for 10 minutes, allowing the steam to build up. As soon as steam starts escaping from the pot, reduce the heat to low and cook for another 12–15 minutes. Remove from the

heat and finish cooking in an oven preheated to 170°C/325°F/Gas Mark 3 for 30 minutes or so.

Remove the lid at the table for maximum impact. The beautiful aromas will waft through the room. Serve with Pomegranate Raita (see page 191) on the side, or as an accompaniment to another curry, such as Lamb Shanks with Saffron and Rosewater (see page 119).

Cook's note
If you're not sure about the thickness of your casserole, you'd be wise to place a heat diffusion mat under it to reduce the direct heat.

NARGISI KOFTA CURRY

This curry reminds me of a bygone era. It was a firm favourite on restaurant menus in India in the 1960s and 1970s but has since fallen out of favour, and you rarely see it now. Part of the reason is that it's a difficult dish to get right and can be tricky to put on a menu. However, it has a celebratory feel to it and used to be served quite frequently in the army officers' mess in India. Essentially the kofta are like Scotch eggs, simmered in a curry sauce. Instead of serving them in the sauce, you could serve them as a kebab on their own.

SERVES 4

For the koftas
6 small eggs
500g (1lb 2oz) lean minced lamb
1 onion, finely chopped
4 garlic cloves, finely chopped
1 1/2 teaspoons salt
1/2 teaspoon garam masala
1 1/2 teaspoons red chilli powder
2 tablespoons Crisp Fried Onions
 (see page 203)
6 cloves, roasted in a dry frying pan and
 then finely ground
1 tablespoon chopped mint
2 tablespoons ghee
3 tablespoons roasted chana dal, ground
 in a spice grinder
2 tablespoons coarse semolina
vegetable or corn oil for deep-frying

For the sauce
6 tablespoons vegetable or corn oil
2 bay leaves
4 cloves
3 onions, finely chopped
5cm (2-inch) piece of fresh ginger, grated

5 garlic cloves, chopped
1 teaspoon salt
2 tablespoons grated fresh coconut
6 large, ripe tomatoes, puréed
3 green chillies, finely chopped
1/2 teaspoon ground turmeric
1 1/2 teaspoons red chilli powder
2 teaspoons ground cumin
1 teaspoon garam masala
350g (1 1/2 cups) plain yoghurt
1 teaspoon rosewater or kewra
 (screw pine essence)
a pinch of saffron strands
2 tablespoons chopped fresh
 coriander

Boil the eggs until just over soft boiled – i.e. put them in a saucepan of cold water, bring to boiling point, then reduce the temperature to a simmer and time them for 4 minutes exactly. The white will be just set and the yolk creamy. Dip the eggs immediately in cold water, then peel and set aside.

To prepare the koftas, mix the mince with all the remaining ingredients except the semolina and oil. Chill for 15–20 minutes, then knead to form a smooth mix. Divide the mince into 6 equal portions. Encase each egg in the mixture, rather like Scotch eggs, making sure there are no holes in the coating. Place on a plate and sprinkle with the semolina.

In a large saucepan or a deep-fat fryer, heat the oil to 160°C/315°F. Add the eggs and cook until evenly coloured all over. Remove from the pan and drain on kitchen paper.

(If you want to serve the koftas without the sauce, finish cooking them in an oven preheated to 180°C/350°F/Gas Mark 4 for 4–6 minutes.)

For the sauce, heat the oil in a heavy-based pan, add the bay leaves and cloves and let them crackle for 30 seconds or so. Add the chopped onions and sauté until golden. Add the ginger and garlic and sauté for 2–3 minutes, then add the salt and coconut and cook, stirring, for 2 minutes. Add the puréed tomatoes, green chillies and all the ground spices, including the garam masala. Simmer over a medium heat for 10–15 minutes until the oil begins to separate from the mixture. Stir in the yoghurt and 1/2 cup of water and cook for 2 minutes. Now add the prepared koftas, folding them in very gently to coat them with the sauce. Reduce the heat and simmer for 4–5 minutes. Finally stir in the rosewater or kewra and saffron and infuse for 2 minutes over a low heat.

Slice the eggs horizontally in half, then return them to the sauce. Garnish with the chopped coriander and serve with rice or chapattis.

Cook's note
Traditionally this dish is made with hard-boiled eggs but I much prefer it with soft-boiled ones. Depending upon availability, you could use duck's eggs or quail's eggs, and even serve these as snacks with the sauce on the side.

LAMB COOKED WITH WINTER VEGETABLES AND SPINACH

SAAG GOSHT

Although made in most of Punjab and northern India, this recipe has its origins in Kashmir, the northernmost state on the border of Pakistan, where the winters are severe. It is a simple yet warming everyday recipe using turnips, carrots and other familiar vegetables. It may well have been the starting point of what is usually known as saag gosht in the Western world, minus the root vegetables, but try it with the vegetables and see the difference for yourself.

SERVES 4

500g (1lb 2oz) spinach leaves
4 tablespoons ghee or vegetable oil
2 teaspoons cumin seeds
1 teaspoon cloves
2 large onions, finely chopped
4 tablespoons finely chopped garlic
4 tablespoons finely chopped fresh ginger
2 teaspoons red chilli powder
2 teaspoons salt
750g (1lb 10oz) boned leg of lamb, cut into 2.5cm (1-inch) cubes
4 green chillies, slit open lengthwise
$^1/_2$ turnip, cut into 1cm ($^1/_2$-inch) cubes
1 carrot, cut into 1cm ($^1/_2$-inch) cubes
300ml (1$^1/_4$ cups) lamb stock or water
2 tomatoes, finely chopped
1 tablespoon gram (chickpea) flour
100g (3$^1/_2$oz) small pickling onions, peeled
1 tablespoon cold butter
juice of $^1/_2$ lemon
1 teaspoon ground spice mix (equal parts of clove, nutmeg, mace and green cardamom, ground in a mortar and pestle)

Blanch the spinach in a large pan of boiling water until wilted, then refresh in cold water and drain. Squeeze out the excess liquid and blitz to a smooth purée in a blender or food processor. Set aside.

Heat the ghee or oil in a large, heavy-based pan and add the cumin and cloves. When they start to crackle, add the chopped onions and sauté until light golden. Add the garlic and ginger and sauté for 2–3 minutes, until the garlic begins to change colour, then add the chilli powder and salt and stir for another couple of minutes, until the spices begin to release their flavour and the fat starts to separate from the mixture.

Now add the lamb pieces and cook over a fairly high heat, stirring constantly, for 8–10 minutes, until the meat begins to brown at the edges. When most of the liquid has evaporated and the lamb is well coloured, stir in the green chillies, turnip and carrot. Add the lamb stock or water, then reduce the heat, cover the pan and cook gently for 30–40 minutes, until the lamb is almost cooked.

Remove the lid, add the tomatoes and cook for 10–12 minutes, until the lamb is cooked through and the tomatoes have been incorporated into the sauce. Add the gram flour and cook, stirring, for a minute, to eliminate any raw flavour. Add the small onions and cook for a minute or two, until glazed but still crunchy. Now add the puréed spinach, increase the heat and stir to mix thoroughly. Check the seasoning, then stir in the butter, lemon juice and spice mix. Serve immediately, with chapattis or other bread.

Cook's notes
Do not cook for too long after adding the spinach purée, or it will discolour and look horrible!

You could substitute diced paneer for the lamb. The cooking time will reduce drastically but the flavours are just as enjoyable.

FIERY RAJASTHANI LAMB CURRY

LAAL MAAS

The name of this dish means 'red meat' in Hindi, indicating the liberal use of dried red chillies that make this dish intensely hot, with robust, smoky flavours.
You could use either lamb or goat – they are interchangeable here. In Rajasthan they would invariably use goat.

This is one of those dishes that contains heat in every sense – it's both 'chilli hot' and 'spice hot'. Cloves and cardamom are effective heat-inducing spices, perfect for cold winter evenings. It's up to you how much heat you'd like in your finished dish. You may discard most of the chilli seeds if you want to reduce the heat, or keep them in if you like it really hot.

SERVES 4

5 tablespoons ghee or vegetable oil
1 teaspoon cloves
25 dried red chillies, stalks removed, broken into 2–3 pieces each and soaked in warm water for 30 minutes
2 bay leaves
6 green cardamom pods
4 black cardamom pods
6½ tablespoons finely chopped garlic
2 large onions, finely chopped
750g (1lb 10oz) lamb (or goat's) leg, cut on the bone into 4cm (1½-inch) dice
600ml (2 cups) water or lamb stock
30g (⅔ cup) fresh coriander, chopped
juice of 1 lemon

For the yoghurt mixture
250g (1 cup) plain yoghurt, whisked until smooth
2 teaspoons cumin seeds, roasted in a dry frying pan
4 teaspoons ground coriander
2 teaspoons red chilli powder
2 teaspoons salt

Mix the yoghurt with the cumin seeds, ground coriander, chilli powder and salt and set aside. Heat 3 tablespoons of the ghee or oil in a large, heavy-based pan. Add the cloves, setting 4–6 aside for later, and 3–4 soaked red chillies, saving the rest for later. Add the bay leaves and the green and black cardamom. When they begin to crackle and change colour, add the garlic and sauté until it starts to turn golden. Add the onions and cook, stirring constantly, until light brown. Now add the meat and cook, stirring, over a high heat for 3–5 minutes. Again, save 3–4 red chillies for later and add the rest to the pan. Cook for 10–12 minutes, until the liquid has evaporated and the meat starts to brown. Add the yoghurt mixture and cook over a medium heat for 15–18 minutes, until the yoghurt has dried up. Pour in the water or lamb stock, then cover the pan, reduce to a simmer and cook for 30 minutes or until the meat is tender. Check the seasoning, remove from the heat and keep warm.

To finish, heat the remaining ghee or oil in a small pan, add the remaining cloves and red chillies and, as they change colour and release their flavours into the fat, pour the mixture over the lamb. Finish with the chopped coriander and lemon juice. This process is called a *tadka*, or tempering, and it boosts the flavours in the dish.

Cook's note
Mixing the ground spices with the yoghurt prevents them getting burnt in the fierce heat of the pan and also thickens the yoghurt, so it doesn't split.

BRAISED SHOULDER OF YOUNG LAMB WITH MINT AND ONION

Most Indian restaurants would use meat from the leg to make a curry but I feel that the shoulder is better suited to this, and it braises really well. This is a typical restaurant dish but I've adapted it so it is simple to do at home.

SERVES 4–6

2 x 1–1.5kg (2¼–3¼lb) shoulders of young lamb
10 green cardamom pods
2 blades of mace
8 cloves, roasted in a dry frying pan
2 x 5cm (2-inch) cinnamon sticks
1 teaspoon royal (black) cumin seeds
2 bay leaves
6 green chillies, slit open lengthwise
800ml water
1 tablespoon vegetable or corn oil
100g (3½oz) small red onions, Madras onions or shallots, peeled
4 tablespoons single cream
1 teaspoon dried fenugreek leaves, crushed between your fingertips
4 tablespoons chopped mint
juice of 1 lemon
½ teaspoon sugar (optional)

For the first marinade
1 tablespoon vegetable or corn oil
juice of 1 lemon
2 teaspoons ground white pepper
1 tablespoon salt
2 tablespoons Ginger-Garlic Paste (see page 202)

For the second marinade
¼ nutmeg, grated
75g (⅓ cup) Fried Cashew Paste (see page 202)

400g (1⅔ cups) Greek-style yoghurt, tied in a muslin cloth and left hanging up overnight to drain
½ teaspoon garam masala
2 tablespoons cream cheese

Trim any surface fat from the lamb shoulders, wash them under cold running water, then drain and pat dry on kitchen paper. Prick each shoulder 4–6 times with the tip of a sharp knife.

Mix together all the ingredients for the first marinade, rub them over the lamb and set aside for 15 minutes.

Mix together all the ingredients for the second marinade and apply them to the shoulders, rubbing and massaging the marinade into the gashes. Place the lamb shoulders in a roasting tray and add the whole spices, bay leaves and 2 of the green chillies. Now pour the water carefully into the tray. Cover with foil and place in an oven preheated to 200°C/400°F/Gas Mark 6. Roast for 30 minutes, then stir the juices and use to baste the meat. Reduce the heat to 170°C/325°F/Gas Mark 3 and cook for 1½ hours. Remove the tray from the oven, take out the meat and let it rest in a warm place for 20 minutes. Pass the cooking juices through a sieve to get rid of the whole spices and set aside.

Heat the oil in a saucepan, add the small onions and sauté for a minute or so, until shiny but still crunchy. Add the remaining green chillies, pour the strained cooking juices into the pan and bring to the boil. Stir in the cream, fenugreek and mint and finish with the lemon juice. Check the seasoning and add the sugar if necessary. Carve the lamb into 4 or 6 pieces, then pour the sauce on top. Serve with a bread of your choice.

LAMB SHANKS WITH SAFFRON AND ROSEWATER

This dish would be made with goat shanks in Lucknow, using the *dum* technique – i.e. cooking the meat in a pot sealed with dough over a very low heat for several hours, allowing the gelatine to be extracted from the bones. It results in a rich, flavourful, full-bodied, smooth sauce, perfumed with rosewater and fortified with saffron.

In India I used to serve 3 shanks per portion – something one can't imagine in the UK. Just one per person will more than suffice!

SERVES 4

4 medium lamb shanks
4 tablespoons vegetable or corn oil
2 black cardamom pods, crushed
2 cinnamon sticks
1 blade of mace
$\frac{1}{2}$ teaspoon cloves
2 onions, cut into quarters
4 tomatoes, cut into quarters
1 bay leaf
2 teaspoons red chilli powder
2 teaspoons Ginger-Garlic Paste
   (see page 202)
$1\frac{1}{2}$ teaspoons salt
$\frac{1}{4}$ teaspoon garam masala

To finish
2 tablespoons single cream
$\frac{1}{2}$ teaspoon sugar
1 tablespoon rosewater
a pinch of saffron strands
$\frac{1}{2}$ teaspoon Mace and Cardamom
   Powder (see page 204)
1 tablespoon chopped fresh coriander

Put the shanks in a large saucepan, cover with cold water and bring to a simmer. Blanch for 5–6 minutes, then drain. Leave until cool enough to handle, then trim off the excess fat, leaving just a thin covering.

Heat a tablespoon of the oil in a heavy-based pan, add the whole spices and let them crackle. Add the onions, tomatoes, bay leaf and a teaspoon of the chilli powder and cook for 4–5 minutes. Pour in 750ml (3 cups) water, bring to a simmer and cook over a fairly high heat for about 20 minutes, till the tomatoes break down completely and the onions are soft. Remove from the heat, blend to a smooth purée in a food processor and then strain.

Heat the remaining oil in a large, heavy-based pan and add the lamb shanks. Cook until light brown all over, then add the ginger-garlic paste and cook for 2–3 minutes longer. Stir in the remaining red chilli powder, plus the salt and the cooked onion and tomato purée. Cook for 5–6 minutes over a moderate heat, then sprinkle in the garam masala. Add 1 litre (4 cups) of water, cover the pan and simmer over a low heat for about 50 minutes, stirring occasionally. Alternatively cover the pan with a tight-fitting lid and place in an oven preheated to 170°C/325°F/Gas Mark 3 for 1–1$\frac{1}{2}$ hours.

When the meat is so tender that it is falling off the bone, remove the shanks from the sauce with a slotted spoon and keep warm. Pass the sauce through a fine sieve into a clean pan, stir in the cream and sugar and simmer until it is thick enough to coat the back of a spoon. Stir in the rosewater, saffron, mace and cardamom powder and chopped coriander. Check the seasoning and remove from the heat. Pour the sauce over the lamb shanks and serve with steamed rice or Pilau Rice (see page 180).

Cook's note
Although in India we cook the shanks on the hob, they come out much better if they are braised in the oven, and better still if you put the pot in the middle of the oven rather than at the bottom.

LAMB CURRY WITH WHITE SPICES

KALIA SAFED

The name of this recipe refers to a lamb dish cooked with white ingredients only or, if other ingredients are used, then they are added in whole form so they can be removed before serving. It used to be one of the many lamb or mutton dishes served as part of any ruler's repast – a white dish using meat was essentially devised to break the monotony of spiced and dark meat dishes. A version of this dish found in Rajasthan is also referred to as *safed maas* – literally meaning 'white meat'.

SERVES 4

800g (1³/₄lb) boned leg of lamb or
  mutton, cut into 4cm (1¹/₂ inch) cubes
50g (¹/₂ cup) broken cashew nuts
1 large onion, roughly chopped
4 tablespoons ghee
2 bay leaves
3 black cardamom pods
1¹/₂ teaspoons white peppercorns
5cm (2-inch) piece of fresh ginger, finely
  grated
1 tablespoon salt
450g (2 cups) Greek-style yoghurt
500ml (2 cups) water
1 teaspoon cloves
2 dried red chillies
1 teaspoon ground green cardamom
1 teaspoon lime juice

Put the meat in a large pan, cover with plenty of cold salted water and bring to the boil. Simmer for 2–3 minutes, then drain. Wash the meat twice in cold water to get rid of any blood.

Put the cashew nuts and onion in a small pan with enough water to cover, bring to the boil and simmer for 15–20 minutes, until tender, skimming any scum from the surface. Blend the mixture to a smooth paste in a food processor or blender, then set aside.

Heat 3 tablespoons of the ghee in a heavy-based pan, add the bay leaves and black cardamom pods and let them crackle. Add the meat, white peppercorns, ginger and salt and cook over a high heat for 5 minutes, stirring frequently. Reduce the heat, add the yoghurt and cook, stirring, until it begins to boil. Add the water, bring to the boil again, then reduce the heat, cover and cook for 30–40 minutes, until the meat is tender. Stir in the cashew and onion paste, cover the pan again and cook gently for 20 minutes.

Heat the remaining tablespoon of ghee in a small pan, add the cloves and red chillies and, as they change colour, tip them into the pan of simmering curry. Finally stir in the green cardamom and finish with the lime juice. Serve with bread or rice of your choice.

Cook's note
You may add various nuts, such as almonds and pistachios, and *khoya* (reduced milk cakes, available from some Indian shops) with the cashew paste if you want to make the curry richer. Some people like to finish it with cream for a smooth, rich sauce. The richer it gets, the closer it becomes to a korma.

LAMB AND BEETROOT CURRY

DO PEEAZA CHUKANDAR

This is a very unusual curry, found mostly in Muslim homes in eastern and central India. The use of beetroot imparts a lovely colour and rich, earthy flavour. It's particularly good for a winter's evening, with Naan Bread (see page 192) or Layered Parathas (see page 196).

SERVES 4

400g (14oz) raw beetroot
750g (1lb 10oz) boned leg of lamb,
  cut into 4cm (1^1/$_2$-inch) cubes
5 tablespoons ghee
1 teaspoon cloves
4 black cardamom pods
3 onions, thinly sliced
2 teaspoons red chilli flakes
500ml (2 cups) water
1 teaspoon garam masala
1 red onion, sliced into rounds
4 sprigs of fresh coriander
juice of ^{1}/$_2$ lemon

For the marinade
150g (^{2}/$_3$ cup) plain yoghurt
1 tablespoon salt
1^1/$_2$ tablespoons red chilli powder
1 tablespoon ground coriander
2 tablespoons Ginger-Garlic Paste (see
  page 202)

Put the beetroot in a large pan, cover with plenty of water and bring to the boil. Reduce the heat, cover and simmer for about an hour, until the beetroot is tender and most of the water has evaporated. Whiz half the beetroot to a smooth paste in a food processor and cut the rest into 2.5cm (1-inch) cubes. Set aside.

Mix together all the ingredients for the marinade, add the meat and set aside for 20 minutes.

Heat 4 tablespoons of the ghee in a heavy-based pan, add the cloves and black cardamom pods and stir for 30 seconds. Add the sliced onions and fry until golden brown. Then add the marinated meat and cook over a high heat for 10 minutes, stirring constantly. Add the chilli flakes and cook for 2 minutes. Pour in the water, reduce the heat and simmer for 30–35 minutes. When the meat is almost cooked and little liquid remains, add the puréed and diced beetroot and cook for another 5 minutes or until the meat is tender. Stir in the garam masala and simmer over a low heat for a further 5 minutes.

Meanwhile, heat the remaining ghee in a frying pan, add the onion rings and sauté briefly for a minute or so.

Remove from the heat and serve garnished with the coriander sprigs and onion rings and finished with a squeeze of lemon.

Cook's note
Adding 2 tablespoons of vinegar when boiling the beetroot gives a nice kick to the dish.

LAMB CURRY WITH GREEN CHILLIES AND MINT

KACCHI MIRCH KA GOSHT

I remember this from my time working at the Gharana restaurant at the Oberoi Grand Hotel in Calcutta. It is such a fine dish, rich and light, zingy and mild, soft and crunchy, fragrant and fresh – all the things one could possibly ask from a great curry. The ingredients are quite similar to a Rezala (see page 137). However, the addition of ingredients at different stages gives a sequence of textures and flavours that lifts a traditional curry.

SERVES 4

750g (1lb 10oz) boned leg of lamb, cut into 2.5cm (1-inch) cubes
1 litre (4 cups) water
2 bay leaves
5 black peppercorns
2 black cardamom pods

For the paste
2 large onions, diced
100g (1 cup) cashew nuts
2 blades of mace
3 green cardamom pods
300ml (1¼ cups) water
200g (scant 1 cup) plain yoghurt

For the gravy
6 tablespoons ghee
2 cloves
3 green cardamom pods
2 tablespoons Ginger-Garlic Paste (see page 202)
1½ teaspoons salt
6–8 green chillies, cut in half
750ml (3 cups) water
4 tablespoons finely chopped mint
¼ teaspoon Mace and Cardamom Powder (see page 204)

1 red onion, diced
1 tablespoon single cream
juice of 1 lemon

Wash the lamb in cold water, then set aside. Put the water, bay leaves, peppercorns and cardamom into a large pan and bring to the boil. Add the meat, bring the water back to the boil and skim off the scum from the surface. Drain through a colander and set the lamb aside. Blanching it in this way helps get rid of any blood in the meat, keeping it light in colour.

Next make the paste. Put the onions, cashew nuts, mace and cardamom in a pan, cover with the water and bring to the boil. Simmer until the onions and nuts are soft, then strain through a sieve. Add the yoghurt to the onion and cashew mixture and blitz in a food processor or blender until smooth.

For the gravy, heat half the ghee in a large, heavy-based pan, add the cloves and cardamom pods and let them crackle. Add the ginger-garlic paste and cook, stirring to prevent sticking, for 3–4 minutes. Add the lamb and sauté for 5 minutes over a high heat without letting it colour. Stir in the salt.

Pour in the cashew and onion paste and stir until the mixture comes to the boil. Add half the green chillies and the water, then cover the pan, reduce the heat and simmer for 35–40 minutes, until the meat is tender. Stir in the mint and mace and cardamom powder, followed by the diced onion and the remaining green chillies and ghee. Simmer for 3–4 minutes, until the onion is cooked but still crunchy. Stir in the cream and lemon juice and serve with steamed rice or Spring Onion Parathas (see page 195).

LAMB ROGAN JOSH

Most restaurants like to use meat from the leg to make a Rogan Josh but it comes out so much better if you use shanks, the sauce shiny and full of flavour from the gelatine. You could use whole shanks, as we do at The Cinnamon Club from time to time, but at home it's easier if the shanks are cut into 3 or 4 pieces, as you would for an *osso buco*. You can ask your butcher to cut them up for you. If you don't want to use lamb, the dish would be just as successful made with mutton or goat.

Not a lot of people know this, but *rogan josh* means 'red juice'. It's a Kashmiri dish, where the redness comes from the bark of a locally grown tree called *rattan jyoth*. It is more than likely that you will not be able to find this even in Asian shops, so I suggest you use crushed beetroot in the final tempering process instead.

SERVES 4

6 lamb shanks, cut into 3 or 4 pieces on the bone
4 tablespoons oil or ghee
2 black cardamom pods, lightly crushed
2 cinnamon sticks
$1/2$ teaspoon black peppercorns
2 large onions, finely chopped
$1^1/2$ teaspoons salt
1 tablespoon Ginger Paste (see page 202)
1 tablespoon Garlic Paste (see page 202)
$1^1/2$ tablespoons Kashmiri chilli powder
$1/2$ teaspoon ground coriander
200g (scant 1 cup) plain yoghurt
500ml (2 cups) lamb stock or water
1 teaspoon ground ginger
$1/2$ teaspoon ground fennel seeds
$1/4$ teaspoon garam masala
2 tablespoons single cream

1 tablespoon chopped fresh coriander

For tempering (optional)
1 tablespoon ghee
2 sticks of rattan jyoth (or $1/2$ raw beetroot, roughly crushed with a rolling pin or meat mallet)

Pat the cut lamb shanks dry on kitchen paper and set aside.

Heat the oil or ghee in a heavy-based casserole, add the crushed cardamom, cinnamon sticks and peppercorns and stir for 30 seconds or so, until they release their flavours into the oil. Add the onions and salt and cook for 10–12 minutes, until the onions are golden brown. Add the ginger and garlic pastes and cook for a couple of minutes, stirring constantly to prevent the pastes sticking to the pan. Now add the lamb and cook, stirring, for 10–12 minutes, until evenly coloured on all sides.

Add the chilli powder and ground coriander and cook for a further 2–3 minutes. Take care to handle the shanks carefully so the meat does not come off the bone at this stage. Gradually whisk in the yoghurt over a low heat until it has all been absorbed, stirring continuously. Add the lamb stock or water, bring to a simmer and cover with a tight-fitting lid. Cook over a low heat for 30–40 minutes, until the meat is tender enough to fall off the bone easily. You could add some more

stock or water if the sauce is too thick or the mixture becomes too dry. Stir in the ground ginger, fennel and garam masala, then cover and set aside for 5 minutes.

For the tempering, heat the ghee in a small pan, tie up the rattan jyoth or beetroot in a square of muslin and add to the ghee. Leave it to infuse for 1 minute. Add the infused ghee and the muslin bag to the lamb shanks and simmer for 2 minutes, until the sauce turns dark red. Remove the meat from the sauce, then add the cream and chopped coriander to bring the sauce back together. Pour the sauce over the meat. Serve with steamed or boiled basmati rice or a bread of your choice.

Cook's notes
Take care not to add the yoghurt all at once, as this will lower the temperature of the sauce and the yoghurt will split.

Although it is not traditional to finish this dish off in the oven, I find the results are better if you do so. It improves the texture, the meat does not get broken up and, what's best if you're entertaining, it frees you up to get on with other things! After adding the water or stock, simply cover the casserole and braise in an oven preheated to 170°C/325°F/Gas Mark 3 for about 2 hours.

MEATBALL CURRY

KHOLA CURRY

This curry comes from the Chettinad region of Tamil Nadu, which is dominated by the Chettiar community, made up predominantly of bankers. The Chettiars made their fortune from labourers in Malaysia in the early nineteenth century and in the process amassed property all over Southeast Asia. They are mainly vegetarian, with meat and fish eaten as a special treat during big celebrations. As a wealthy community, it was the norm for them to hire help to assist *Archi* (the lady of the house) with cooking and cleaning. These cooks were not vegetarian, and Khola Curry was one of the many dishes they introduced into Chettiar homes.

SERVES 4

For the meatballs
500g (1lb 2oz) minced lamb
8 green chillies, roughly chopped
8 garlic cloves, roughly chopped
1/3 coconut, inner brown skin removed, flesh finely grated
80g (scant 1 cup) cashew nuts, lightly roasted in a dry frying pan
60g (1/3 cup) roasted chana dal
2 tablespoons each of poppy seeds and fennel seeds, roasted in a dry frying pan
5 shallots, roughly chopped
1 1/2 teaspoons ground turmeric
5cm (2-inch) piece of fresh ginger, roughly chopped
2 teaspoons salt

For the sauce
100ml (scant 1/2 cup) vegetable or corn oil
7.5cm (3-inch) piece of cinnamon stick
4 bay leaves
2 tablespoons fennel seeds
15 shallots, finely chopped
3 sprigs of fresh curry leaves
3 tablespoons Ginger-Garlic Paste (see page 202)
3 large tomatoes, diced
2 1/2 teaspoons red chilli powder
2 tablespoons ground coriander
1 teaspoon ground turmeric
500ml (2 cups) water or lamb stock
2 teaspoons salt

Blitz all the ingredients for the meatballs together in a food processor, or mince them in a mincer. Check the seasoning by frying a teaspoon or so of the mixture and tasting it. Divide into small balls (slightly smaller than golf balls) and leave in the fridge while you make the sauce.

Heat the oil in a heavy-based pan, add the cinnamon, bay leaves and fennel seeds and cook for about 30 seconds, until they crackle. Add the shallots and curry leaves and fry for 8–10 minutes, until the shallots are golden. Add the ginger-garlic paste and sauté for 2–3 minutes, then stir in the tomatoes and cook for 5 minutes. Stir in all the ground spices. Add the water or stock and salt, bring to the boil and simmer over a medium heat for 12–15 minutes, till the oil separates from the sauce. Add the meatballs to the sauce and simmer for 5–8 minutes, until just cooked through. Check the seasoning and serve immediately, with either Layered Parathas (see page 196) or Pilau Rice (see page 180).

Cook's notes
When you've removed the mince from the food processor, rinse out the processor with 500ml (2 cups) water and use this to cook the sauce rather than plain water; there's much more flavour.

You may need to oil the palms of your hands when shaping the meatballs, to prevent them sticking.

MUGHAL-STYLE AROMATIC CURRY OF LAMB SHANKS

NALLI KORMA

This recipe comes from the Awadh region of India. In the Mughal courts of Lucknow, such delicate dishes of slow-cooked meat with fragrant spicing were the norm. I find lamb shoulder shanks best for this dish, as the meat is lighter and less fibrous than leg shanks. In India, the shanks are smaller than the ones in the West and we use goat shanks instead of lamb.

SERVES 3

6 lamb shoulder shanks, French trimmed
1.5 litres (6 cups) water
5 tablespoons vegetable or corn oil
50g ($^1/_2$ cup) cashew nuts
4 onions, finely sliced
125ml ($^1/_2$ cup) water
2 bay leaves
3 green cardamom pods
2.5cm (1-inch) piece of cinnamon stick
1 tablespoon chopped fresh ginger
1 tablespoon chopped garlic
4 green chillies, chopped
2 teaspoons ground coriander
1 teaspoon red chilli powder
1 teaspoon salt
1 teaspoon garam masala
3 tablespoons plain yoghurt
$^1/_2$ teaspoon ground mace
$^1/_3$ teaspoon ground cardamom

For the marinade
1 tablespoon Ginger Paste (see page 202)
1 tablespoon Garlic Paste (see page 202)
1 teaspoon salt

To finish
a generous pinch of saffron strands

2 teaspoons kewra (screw pine essence)
or rosewater
juice of 1 lime
3 tablespoons single cream

Put the shanks in a large pan, cover with the water and bring to the boil, then drain. Leave the shanks to cool, then trim off any surface fat.

Mix together the marinade ingredients, rub them over the lamb shanks and leave to marinate for 20 minutes. Infuse the saffron in the kewra or rosewater and set aside.

Heat half the oil in a heavy-based pan, add the cashew nuts and sauté until golden. Remove with a slotted spoon, allowing the oil to drain back into the pan, then set the nuts aside to cool. Fry the onions in the oil until golden brown, then remove with a slotted spoon and spread out on a tray to cool. Put the cashew nuts and onions in a blender and blitz to a paste, gradually adding the water.

Heat the remaining oil in a large, heavy-based pan, add the bay leaves, cardamom and cinnamon and let them crackle. Add the ginger, garlic and green chillies and sauté for 2 minutes. Now add the lamb, raise the heat and stir-fry until golden brown. Add the ground coriander, red chilli powder, salt and half the garam masala and cook, stirring, for 2 minutes. Add the yoghurt and cook over a high heat, stirring constantly, for 8–10 minutes, until it has been completely absorbed.

Now add the fried onion and cashew nut paste, the remaining garam masala and the ground mace and cardamom. Pour in enough water just to cover, bring to a simmer, then cover and cook for 40 minutes, until the meat is tender. Adjust the seasoning and finish with the lime juice, cream and the saffron mixture. Serve with Pilau Rice (see page 180) or Layered Parathas (see page 196).

Cook's note
You could braise the shanks in a sealed pot in a moderate oven for an hour or so after adding the water. This will ensure a slow release of gelatine. If the sauce is too thin, remove the shanks and simmer the sauce until it reduces and thickens enough to coat the back of a spoon. Finish with the lime juice, cream and saffron mixture.

DECCAN LAMB COOKED WITH LENTILS

DAL GOSHT

This is quite popular in the Deccan region, where it is thought to have originated from the kitchens of the Nizam, the rulers of Hyderabad. Also referred to as *dalcha*, it makes a great winter dish.

SERVES 4

750g (1lb 10oz) boned lamb, cut into 2.5cm (1-inch) cubes
200g (1 cup) chana dal (split yellow peas)
2 black cardamom pods
1 teaspoon ground turmeric
1 litre (4 cups) water
1 1/2 teaspoons salt
4 tablespoons vegetable or corn oil
4 cloves
4 green cardamom pods
5cm (2-inch) piece of cinnamon stick
4 black peppercorns
1 bay leaf
4 onions, finely chopped
1 tablespoon Ginger-Garlic Paste (see page 202)
3 tomatoes, cut into quarters
10 fresh curry leaves
1 tablespoon tamarind paste
1/2 teaspoon garam masala
1 tablespoon chopped fresh coriander
2 teaspoons desiccated coconut
juice of 1/2 lime
a pinch of sugar

For the fresh spice mix
5 tablespoons coriander stalks
3 garlic cloves, roughly chopped
4 green chillies, roughly chopped
1/2 teaspoon coriander seeds, roasted in a dry frying pan

1/2 teaspoon cumin seeds, roasted in a dry frying pan
1/2 tablespoon vegetable or corn oil

Wash the lamb in cold running water, then drain and pat dry on kitchen paper. Set aside.

Blend all the ingredients for the fresh spice mix to a coarse paste in a small food processor and set aside.

Wash the chana dal and place in a heavy-based pan with the black cardamom pods, turmeric, water and 1/2 teaspoon of the salt. Bring to the boil and simmer for 30 minutes, until about three-quarters cooked. Remove from the heat and keep warm.

Meanwhile, heat the oil in another heavy-based pan, add the whole spices and the bay leaf and let them crackle for a minute or so. Add the onions and sauté for 8–10 minutes, until golden. Add the ginger-garlic paste and stir for a minute, then add the lamb, the remaining salt and 2 tablespoons of the fresh spice mix. Cook over a high heat, stirring constantly, for 6–8 minutes, until the lamb colours lightly. Drop the tomato quarters into the pan and cook for 3 minutes, until softened. Pour in 250ml (1 cup) water, reduce the heat and cover the pan. Simmer for 45 minutes, until the lamb is almost cooked.

Now pour in the chana dal and its cooking liquid and continue to cook for 6–8 minutes, until the

lamb is tender. Stir in the fresh curry leaves, garam masala and tamarind paste, then reduce the heat and simmer for 2–3 minutes. Finish the dish with the chopped coriander, coconut, lime juice and sugar. Serve with steamed rice or Pilau Rice (see page 180).

PUNJABI-SPICED MUTTON CHOPS AND MINCE

RARHA MUTTON CHAAMP

This dish is typical of the rustic, Punjabi-style cooking that has been made popular by *dhabas*, or roadside cafés, which traditionally cater to the truck drivers who drive the length and breadth of the country, carrying goods of all types. The success of these *dhabas* is a testimony to the business acumen and adaptability of the Punjabis, who saw this opportunity as the majority of Indian truck drivers happen to be from Punjab.

SERVES 4

1 teaspoon Ginger Paste (see page 202)
1 teaspoon Garlic Paste (see page 202)
1 teaspoon ground cumin
2 teaspoons ground coriander
120g (1/2 cup) plain yoghurt
125ml (1/2 cup) water
3 tablespoons ghee
2 bay leaves
3 cloves
2 cardamom pods
2.5cm (1-inch) piece of cinnamon stick
5 black peppercorns
4 onions, finely sliced
8-bone mutton rack, French trimmed
  and cut into individual cutlets (ask
  your butcher to do this)
2 teaspoons salt
250g (9oz) minced mutton
2 teaspoons red chilli powder
3 ripe tomatoes, puréed
3 green chillies, finely chopped
5cm (2-inch) piece of fresh ginger, cut
  into thin strips
1/4 teaspoon garam masala
4 tablespoons chopped fresh coriander
juice of 1 lemon

In a bowl, mix the ginger and garlic pastes, cumin, coriander, yoghurt and water together and set aside. Heat the ghee in a large, heavy-based saucepan, add the bay leaves, cloves, cardamom, cinnamon and peppercorns and let them crackle. Add the onions and stir-fry until golden brown. Add the mutton cutlets and stir-fry over a high heat for 6–8 minutes, allowing them to turn an even brown. Add the salt and stir-fry for another 2 minutes, then reduce the heat and remove the cutlets from the pan.

Add the mince to the pan, raise the heat and cook, stirring, for 3–4 minutes. Pour in the yoghurt mixture and stir over a high heat for 8–10 minutes, until the mince is cooked and the yoghurt has dried out. Now add the chilli powder and puréed tomatoes and cook over a medium heat for 5 minutes, until the tomatoes are thoroughly incorporated.

Return the cutlets to the pan and cook for 6–8 minutes, until they are cooked through and coated in the mince mixture. Stir in the green chillies, ginger and garam masala and finish with the chopped coriander and lemon juice. Serve with Layered Parathas (see page 196) or Naan Bread (see page 192).

Cook's note
If the mince isn't cooked by the time the yoghurt has dried out, add about 250ml (1 cup) water and continue cooking.

MUTTON COOKED WITH LENTILS, DRIED FRUIT AND NUTS

HAREESA

This dish would originally have been made with camel meat and you could still use that if you are able to find any! The recipe comes from the Deccan region of India. The nomadic tribes that used to cook it would often serve it as a complete meal, containing rice, lentils and meat all in one. On cold winter nights, the savoury porridge would cook for hours over a slow-burning wood fire and its flavours would be rich and creamy.

SERVES 4

5 tablespoons ghee
$\frac{1}{2}$ teaspoon cloves
5cm (2-inch) piece of cinnamon stick
5 green cardamom pods
$\frac{1}{2}$ teaspoon black peppercorns
2 large onions, finely sliced
6 garlic cloves, finely chopped
1 teaspoon ground turmeric
1 tablespoon red chilli flakes
2 teaspoons salt
750g (1lb 10oz) lean mutton from the leg, cut into thin strips
2 litres (8 cups) water
150g ($\frac{3}{4}$ cup) masoor dal (red lentils)
50g ($\frac{1}{2}$ cup) basmati rice
125g plain yoghurt
5cm (2-inch) piece of fresh ginger, chopped
6 green chillies, slit open lengthwise
1 tablespoon coriander seeds, roasted in a dry frying pan and coarsely ground
1 tablespoon cumin seeds, roasted in a dry frying pan and coarsely ground
1 tablespoon fennel seeds, roasted in a dry frying pan and coarsely ground
125ml ($\frac{1}{2}$ cup) single cream
50g ($\frac{1}{2}$ cup) almonds and pistachios, chopped
1 tablespoon raisins
2 tablespoons chopped mint

Heat 4 tablespoons of the ghee in a large, heavy-based pan and add the cloves, cinnamon stick, cardamom pods and black peppercorns. Let them crackle, then add the onions and sauté until golden brown. Add the garlic and sauté for another couple of minutes, then stir in the turmeric, red chilli flakes and salt. Add the meat and cook, stirring, over a high heat for 15 minutes. Pour in the water, bring to the boil, then reduce the heat and simmer for 20–25 minutes, until the meat is nearly half cooked. Then add the lentils and rice and cook for another 20–25 minutes, until the meat, rice and lentils are all tender and most of the water has been absorbed.

Gradually stir in the yoghurt, then add the ginger, green chillies and ground roasted seeds. Cook over a medium heat for 10 minutes. Stir in the cream and cook for 3 minutes longer.

Heat the remaining tablespoon of ghee in a separate pan, add the almonds, pistachios and raisins and fry lightly for a couple of minutes. Stir in the mint and pour it all on to the porridge. Check the seasoning and serve immediately, with vegetables of your choice.

Cook's note
You could cook this dish with venison, water buffalo or any similar lean meat.

RAJASTHANI SEMI-DRY CURRY WITH MUTTON

HANDI BOOTHA

This Rajasthani speciality is often served as an appetiser, even though it's actually a curry. It's quite a dry dish, with rich, intense flavours, and is similar to a *kosha mangsho* (a rich but dry lamb curry from Bengal), and even the ever-popular *bhuna*, served in Indian restaurants across the UK. The inclusion of onions and tomatoes adds colour and texture to the dish and lightens it up.

SERVES 4

800g (1³/₄lb) boned leg of mutton, cut into 4cm (1¹/₂-inch) cubes
3 tablespoons vegetable or corn oil, or mustard oil
3 onions, finely chopped
4 tomatoes, puréed
500ml (2 cups) water

For the marinade
240g (1 cup) plain yoghurt
2 dried red chillies
5 cloves
3 green cardamom pods
¹/₂ teaspoon black peppercorns
2.5cm (1-inch) piece of cinnamon stick
2 bay leaves
5cm (2-inch) piece of fresh ginger, grated
3 garlic cloves, chopped
1 tablespoon red chilli powder
1 tablespoon ground cumin
1 tablespoon ground coriander
2 teaspoons salt

To finish the dish
1 tablespoon ghee
1 teaspoon cumin seeds
3 garlic cloves, chopped
2 onions, cut into 2.5cm (1-inch) dice
2 tomatoes, deseeded and diced

¹/₂ teaspoon garam masala
100g (2 cups) fresh coriander, chopped
¹/₂ teaspoon sugar
juice of ¹/₂ lemon

Wash the diced mutton under cold running water, then drain and pat dry on kitchen paper. Mix together all the ingredients for the marinade, add the meat and set aside for 15–20 minutes.

In the meantime, heat the oil in a large, heavy-based pan, add the chopped onions and sauté over a medium heat until brown. Add the marinated meat and stir over a high heat for 10–12 minutes, until the edges of the meat start to brown. Cook for a further 6 minutes or until the juices have dried up. Now add the tomatoes and cook over a high heat for 5–6 minutes. Add the water, cover the pan and simmer gently for 20–25 minutes, stirring occasionally, until the meat is tender. Remove from the heat and set aside.

In a separate large pan, heat the ghee, add the cumin seeds and garlic and sauté until golden. Add the diced onions and sauté until they are shiny but still crisp. Add the cooked mutton mixture and stir-fry over a high heat until the spices coat the pieces of meat and the moisture dries up. Add the tomatoes, garam masala and coriander and stir for a minute or two, taking care that the tomatoes and onions don't

disintegrate. Check the seasoning, add the sugar and finish with the lemon juice. Serve with Layered Parathas (see page 196).

Cook's note
The initial cooking of the mutton can be done a day in advance. It is easier to stir-fry if it is cold.

THIS CURRY REMINDS ME OF AN ERA GONE BY
IT WAS A FIRM FAVOURITE ON RESTAURANT.
MENUS IN INDIA IN THE 1960S AND 1970S
BUT HAS SINCE FALLEN OUT OF FAVOUR,
AND YOU RARELY SEE IT NOW.'

NARGISI KOFTA CURRY, PAGE 110

MUTTON KOLHAPURI

The cooking in Maharashtra can be broadly divided into two categories: Konkani, the food of the coastal region, and Malwani, the food of the landlocked interiors. Malwani cooking is earthy and rustic, based on fiery spices and coarse spice pastes. Kolhapur is a small town in Maharashtra, which has popularised this Malwani curry.

SERVES 4–6

2 tablespoons vegetable or corn oil
2 dried bay leaves
5 dried red chillies
8 cloves
4 x 2.5cm (1-inch) pieces of cinnamon stick
4 red onions, chopped
1kg (2¼lb) boned leg of mutton (or lamb), cut into 2.5cm (1-inch) cubes
2 tablespoons red chilli powder
1 teaspoon ground turmeric
1 tablespoon salt
5 tomatoes, finely chopped
1 litre (4 cups) water
2 teaspoons garam masala
1 tablespoon chopped fresh coriander

For the roasted spice blend (Kolhapur masala)
1 teaspoon black peppercorns
2 blades of mace
2 teaspoons coriander seeds
2 teaspoons cumin seeds
2 tablespoons fennel seeds
2 tablespoons sesame seeds
1 tablespoon melon seeds (available in Asian stores)
2 teaspoons poppy seeds
2 tablespoons desiccated coconut
4 garlic cloves, chopped

7.5cm (3-inch) piece of fresh ginger, chopped

First prepare the spice blend. Roast the spices, seeds and coconut in a dry frying pan over a low heat for 4–5 minutes. Remove from the heat and grind to a paste with the garlic and ginger, adding a little water as needed.

Heat the oil in a large, heavy-based pan with a heavy lid, add the bay leaves, whole red chillies, cloves and cinnamon sticks and let them crackle for 30 seconds or so. Add the onions and sauté till golden brown.
Stir in the mutton and cook for 10–12 minutes, until browned, then mix in the chilli powder, turmeric, roasted spice blend and salt.
Cook for a good 5–8 minutes, stirring frequently to prevent the paste catching on the bottom of the pan.

Add the tomatoes and cook over a high heat for 10 minutes. Pour in the water, bring to a simmer, then reduce the heat and cover the pan. Simmer for 45 minutes–1 hour, until the mutton is tender. Add the garam masala and check the seasoning. Stir in the chopped coriander and serve with rice or bread of your choice.

BHOPAL-STYLE GOAT CURRY

REZALA

Many regions claim this dish originated in their area but it was the Begum of Bhopal who made it the most popular. I like it, as it's simple to make and very easy to remember. Strangely, it resembles a pound cake recipe, where you use equal quantities of everything and mix them up and bang them in the oven to get a cake! In this case, just mix together all the ingredients and seal the pot. Cook either on the hob over a very low heat or in the oven at 150°C/300°F/Gas Mark 2 for 2 hours. Beware though – the dish may have quite a kick, depending upon which type of green chilli you use.

SERVES 4

1kg (2¼lb) goat's meat from the leg, cut into 2.5cm (1-inch) cubes
200ml (scant 1 cup) vegetable oil or ghee
2 x quantity of Crisp Fried Onions (see page 203), coarsely crushed
200g (scant 1 cup) Greek-style yoghurt
200ml (scant 1 cup) water
25 green chillies, slit open lengthwise and deseeded
25g (1oz) piece of fresh pineapple, blended in a mini chopper or finely grated
4 tablespoons roasted gram (chickpea) flour
4 teaspoons salt
2 tablespoons finely chopped fresh ginger
1 tablespoon Garlic Paste (see page 202)
1 teaspoon allspice
2 teaspoons cumin seeds
4 black cardamom pods
2 teaspoons garam masala

To seal
250g (1⅔ cup) plain flour
125ml (½ cup) water

To finish
100ml (scant ½ cup) single cream
1 tablespoon cashew nuts, fried in a little oil until golden
100g (2 cups) fresh coriander, chopped
juice of 1 lemon
1 tablespoon chopped mint

Mix the meat with all the other ingredients and set aside for 10–15 minutes.

Choose an earthenware casserole or a heavy-based pan with a tight-fitting lid. Place the marinated meat in the pot. Mix together the flour and water to make a dough for sealing the lid and stretch it into a thin strip, long enough to cover the edge of the lid all the way round. Stick the dough on to the edge of the lid and place it on the casserole, pressing lightly to make sure that it is completely sealed. Place the pan over a low heat and cook for 2 hours. Remove the lid and check to see if the meat is done; if not, simply cover again and cook until it is tender. Stir the sauce and finish by adding the cream, plus another couple of tablespoons of water if necessary to loosen it. Bring to the boil, check the seasoning and correct if required. Sprinkle with the fried cashew nuts, chopped coriander, lemon juice and mint and serve immediately.

Cook's note
You could substitute mutton or hogget for the goat and, if your butcher cuts the meat into escalopes, you could try using these rather than diced meat. It will reduce the cooking time by almost half and taste just as good. Cuts from the neck or shoulder also work well in this kind of dish.

BEEF BHUNA, BENGALI STYLE

Bhuna is a term you commonly find on restaurant menus. It refers to cooking meat with spices with little or no water added. This requires constant stirring to prevent the spices sticking to the bottom of the pan but the resulting dish is rich and intense in flavour from the caramelisation of the onions and the frying of the spices. I've made things easier here by adding a little water but do make sure that all or most of it dries up so there is no loss of flavour.

SERVES 4–6

750g (1lb 10oz) boneless beef chuck
   steak, cut into 4cm (1$^{1}/_{2}$-inch) cubes
3 tablespoons ghee
$^{1}/_{2}$ teaspoon cloves
2 green cardamom pods
1 black cardamom pod
$^{1}/_{2}$ teaspoon black peppercorns
2 bay leaves
3 green chillies, slit lengthwise in half
250ml (1 cup) water
2 tomatoes, finely chopped
2.5cm (1-inch) piece of fresh ginger,
   finely chopped
3 tablespoons tamarind paste
juice of $^{1}/_{2}$ lemon
2 tablespoons chopped fresh coriander
a pinch of sugar

For the marinade
2 onions, finely chopped
3 tablespoons Ginger-Garlic Paste (see
   page 202)
2 teaspoons salt
2 teaspoons red chilli powder
2 teaspoons cumin seeds, roasted in a
   dry frying pan and then ground
2 teaspoons ground coriander
$^{1}/_{2}$ teaspoon ground turmeric

Mix together all the ingredients for the marinade. Add the beef, turning to coat it well, and set aside for 30 minutes.

Heat the ghee in a large, heavy-based pan, add the whole spices and bay leaves and let them splutter. Add the marinated meat and stir well over a high heat, until the juices are absorbed and the meat begins to brown. Add the green chillies and water, then reduce the heat, cover and cook gently for 25–30 minutes, until the beef is about two-thirds done. Add the tomatoes and ginger and cook for 8–10 minutes over a high heat, stirring all the time to mash up the tomatoes. You may have to add a couple of tablespoons of water to prevent the sauce sticking to the bottom of the pan.

When fat begins to leave the side of the pan, the meat has reached the bhuna stage. Now stir in the tamarind paste and lemon juice, followed by the chopped coriander. Finally add the pinch of sugar, then cover the pan and switch off the heat. Leave for about 5 minutes so the meat can complete the cooking in its own heat. Serve with Layered Parathas (see page 196).

SPICE-CRUSTED RIB EYE STEAK WITH MASALA SAUTÉED POTATOES

Steak and chips, I suppose! This is, of course, a purely concocted dish, drawing inspiration from the all-time favourite way of enjoying good meat. All I have done is spice things up a little, being careful not to let the spices overpower the main element and detract from the enjoyment of the meat. The semi-dry spice crust on the steak provides a balance of textures and serves as both crust and sauce.

SERVES 4

4 x 200g (7oz) rib eye steaks
1 tablespoon vegetable or corn oil
chopped chives, to garnish

For the marinade
1 teaspoon red chilli powder
$^1/_2$ teaspoon salt
1 tablespoon vegetable or corn oil

For the spice crust
2 tablespoons vegetable or corn oil
1 large onion, finely chopped
1 teaspoon salt
2.5cm (1-inch) piece of fresh ginger, finely chopped
1 teaspoon red chilli powder
3 tomatoes, finely chopped
1 teaspoon red chilli flakes
1 teaspoon coriander seeds, crushed
1 teaspoon fennel seeds, crushed

For the masala sautéed potatoes
4 medium-sized starchy potatoes, such as Maris Piper, peeled and cut into slices about 5mm ($^1/_4$ inch) thick
2 teaspoons salt
1 teaspoon ground turmeric
2 tablespoons vegetable or corn oil

1 teaspoon cumin seeds
1 large onion, finely chopped
$^1/_2$ teaspoon red chilli powder
1 teaspoon ground cumin
1 teaspoon salt
1 red onion, sliced into rings
1 tomato, deseeded and diced
1cm ($^1/_2$-inch) piece of fresh ginger, finely chopped
1 tablespoon chopped fresh coriander
2 green chillies, finely chopped

Mix together the ingredients for the marinade, rub them over the steaks and set aside.

To make the spice crust, heat the oil in a heavy-based pan, add the onion and sauté over a high heat for 2–3 minutes. Add the salt, reduce the heat, then cover and cook for 15–20 minutes, until the onion is soft and disintegrated. Add the ginger, chilli powder and tomatoes and cook, stirring, for 3–5 minutes, until the tomatoes have reduced and the mixture becomes quite dry. Stir in the chilli flakes, coriander seeds and fennel seeds, then remove from the heat and set aside.

For the masala sautéed potatoes, blanch the potato slices by simmering them in a pan of boiling water with the salt and half the turmeric for 2–3 minutes, then drain well. Heat the oil in a large, heavy-based frying pan and add the cumin seeds. When they start to crackle, add the chopped onion and sauté until golden brown. Add the remaining turmeric

and the blanched potatoes to the pan and sauté over a medium heat until the potatoes start to crisp up around the edges. Now stir in the chilli powder, cumin and salt, add the onion rings and diced tomato and cook, stirring, for 2 minutes. Sprinkle in the ginger, coriander and green chillies and cook for 2–3 minutes, until the onion rings start to wilt and the potatoes are crisp.

To cook the steaks, heat the oil in a large, heavy-based frying pan, add the steaks and sear them for 2–3 minutes on each side for medium rare (if you prefer your meat more cooked, place it in an oven preheated to 180°C/350°F/Gas Mark 4 to obtain the desired degree of doneness). Leave to rest for 2–3 minutes. Spoon the spice crust over the steaks and place under a hot grill for a minute or two, until it begins to colour.

Divide the potatoes between 4 plates, put the steak on top, garnish with chives and serve immediately.

Cook's note
The spice crust for the steak can be made well in advance.

The method for the sautéed potatoes is quite similar to the French one, where the potatoes are cut thick and fried over a fairly slow heat for even cooking and a crisp texture. You may also add a pinch of dried thyme for extra depth of flavour, if you like.

ROAST PORK CHOPS WITH SWEET SPICES, MUSTARD MASH AND DATE AND CHILLI SAUCE

This may seem an unusual combination but the flavours and textures complement each other brilliantly. I consider this to be one of the joys of modern cooking – the sense of liberation you get from combining a Bengali-style mustard mash with sweet spiced pork plus a date and chilli sauce inspired by an Indian chutney. Enjoy the freedom!

SERVES 4

4 pork chops, trimmed
2 tablespoons vegetable or corn oil

For the date and chilli sauce
100g ($^3/_4$ cup) dried dates
4 garlic cloves, chopped
5 dried red chillies, broken into 2–3 pieces each
2.5cm (1-inch) piece of fresh ginger, chopped
1.5 litres (6 cups) chicken stock or water
2 tablespoons soy sauce
2 tablespoons balsamic vinegar
$^1/_2$ teaspoon salt
1 teaspoon sugar

For the spice rub
1 teaspoon black peppercorns
$^1/_4$ nutmeg
$^1/_2$ teaspoon cloves
2 blades of mace
1 teaspoon green cardamom pods
2.5cm (1-inch) piece of fresh galangal, chopped
$^1/_2$ teaspoon allspice berries
2.5cm (1-inch) piece of fresh ginger, chopped
$^1/_2$ teaspoon ground turmeric
2 teaspoons fennel seeds
$^1/_4$ teaspoon dried lavender

5cm (2-inch) piece of cinnamon stick
1 teaspoon salt
1 teaspoon red chilli flakes

For the mustard mash
500g (1lb 2oz) floury potatoes such as Desiree, peeled and cut into chunks
$^1/_2$ teaspoon ground turmeric
1 teaspoon salt
100g (scant $^1/_2$ cup) butter
1 tablespoon vegetable or corn oil
$^1/_2$ teaspoon mustard seeds
2 green chillies, chopped
2 tablespoons Dijon or English mustard
2 tablespoons single cream
1 tablespoon chopped fresh coriander

For the sauce, put the dates, garlic, chillies, ginger and stock or water in a saucepan along with any pork trimmings and bring to a simmer. Reduce the heat and cook for 15–20 minutes, until the dates are tender. Remove from the heat and blend with a hand-held blender to give a smooth sauce. Strain through a fine sieve into a clean pan and return to the heat. Bring to a simmer, add the soy sauce, balsamic vinegar, salt and sugar and simmer until it has reduced and thickened enough to coat the back of a spoon and gets a glaze. Remove from the heat and set aside.

To make the spice rub, spread all the ingredients out on a baking tray and place in a very low oven for about 15 minutes, until completely dried out but not burned. Pound them to a coarse powder in a mortar and pestle and rub the mixture over the pork chops. Set aside for 10 minutes.

For the mash, boil the potatoes with the turmeric and salt until tender. Drain and push through a fine sieve, then mix with the butter. Heat the oil in a heavy-based frying pan, add the mustard seeds and let them crackle. Add the green chillies, then stir in the mashed potatoes, add the mustard and cream and cook until the mixture leaves the side of the pan. Stir in the coriander and remove from the heat.

To cook the pork chops, heat the 2 tablespoons of oil in a large, ovenproof frying pan and sear the chops for 3–4 minutes on each side, until they have a crisp skin and a good brown colour. Transfer the pan to an oven preheated to 200°C/400°F/Gas Mark 6 for 4–5 minutes or so to cook through.

To serve, divide the mash between 4 plates, sit the chops on top and pour the sauce around.

Cook's note
If you can obtain the Moroccan spice mix, *ras-el-hanout*, you could use that for the spice rub instead of roasting and grinding your own – just add a few coarsely crushed spices to it, such as fennel, cumin and coriander, and some chilli flakes.

COORG PORK STIR-FRY

PANDHI CURRY

This dish comes from the Coorg region of Karnataka. A pleasant hill station perched in the Western Ghats, Coorg is often referred to as the Scotland of India and is rich in wildlife. The Kodava people were avid hunters in years gone by. The local wild boar provided them with easy pickings and became a staple food, marking the beginnings of the famous Pandhi Curry. Today, many Kodava families have their own pigs and this remains one of their favourite dishes. The meat is cooked twice – first braised slowly until tender, then stir-fried to finish the dish. The high heat during the second cooking caramelises the onions and meat, adding a depth of flavour. This double-cooking technique is also found in certain Bengali-style *bhunas*.

SERVES 4

750g (1lb 10oz) pork loin, cut into 4cm (1½-inch) cubes

For the marinade
2 tablespoons Ginger-Garlic Paste (see page 202)
1 teaspoon ground turmeric
2 teaspoons salt
8–10 black peppercorns
3 bay leaves
4 tablespoons honey
3 tablespoons soy sauce
10 kokum berries, soaked in 100ml (scant ½ cup) hot water for 30 minutes

For the stir-fry
2 tablespoons vegetable or corn oil
4 dried red chillies
10 fresh curry leaves
4 red onions, sliced

Mix together all the ingredients for the marinade, including the soaking water from the kokum berries. Add the pork and leave to marinate in the fridge overnight.

The next day, transfer the pork to a heavy-based saucepan and add just enough water to cover. Bring to a simmer and cook, covered, for 1 hour or until the pork is very tender. Drain the meat, reserving the liquid.

Heat the oil for the stir-fry in a large frying pan or wok and add the dried red chillies. Let them darken, then add the curry leaves and fry for 30 seconds or so, until they start to crisp up. Now add the sliced red onions and sauté until translucent. Add the drained pork and cook, stirring constantly, for 6–8 minutes, until caramelised. Add a tablespoon or two of the reserved cooking liquid and continue to cook until it has evaporated. The meat will acquire a shiny glaze. Correct the seasoning and serve with steamed rice.

Cook's notes
Use as little water as possible to cook the pork first time around. The liquid will have stronger flavours when you can add it to the stir-fry later.

Keep the seasoning slightly milder than you'd like to end up with, as the prolonged cooking makes the final flavour very intense.

PORK VINDALOO

This is probably one of the best-known Indian dishes across the world and also one of the most misunderstood. A lot of people think it's a dish of pork cooked with potatoes, and even in India many restaurants serve it as that. On the contrary, Vindaloo gets its name from vinegar and garlic – two ingredients widely used by the Portuguese, who colonised Goa for many years before it became independent. Vindaloo is also notoriously classed as a fiery dish loaded with chillies. Although this can be true to an extent, most of the heat in the dish comes from peppercorns, cloves and other spices rather than just a one-dimensional hit of chilli.

SERVES 4

4 tablespoons white vinegar
1 tablespoon malt vinegar
800g (1³/₄lb) leg of pork, cut into 2.5cm (1-inch) cubes, with a few pieces left on the bone
4 tablespoons vegetable or corn oil
2 onions, finely sliced
10 garlic cloves, finely sliced
5cm (2-inch) piece of fresh ginger, cut into thin strips
3 ripe tomatoes
1 teaspoon red chilli powder
4 green chillies, chopped
1 teaspoon salt
250ml (1 cup) water
1 teaspoon jaggery or brown sugar

For the masala
seeds from 6 cardamom pods
1 teaspoon black peppercorns
4 dried chillies
6 cloves
5cm (2-inch) piece of cinnamon stick
1 teaspoon cumin seeds
¹/₂ teaspoon coriander seeds
¹/₂ teaspoon fenugreek seeds
¹/₂ teaspoon ground turmeric

First make the masala. Grind all the ingredients together in a clean coffee grinder or spice grinder, or use a mortar and pestle. Mix the ground spices with the vinegars, then add the pork and mix until thoroughly coated. Leave to marinate in the fridge for at least 3 hours.

Heat the oil in a heavy-based pan, add the onions and fry over a low heat until golden brown. Add the garlic, ginger, tomatoes, chilli powder and green chillies and stir well. Increase the heat, add the pork, leaving any marinade behind in the bowl, and stir-fry for 8–12 minutes, until browned all over. Add the salt, water and any leftover marinade, then reduce the heat and slowly bring to the boil. Stir in the jaggery or sugar, cover with a tight-fitting lid and simmer for 45 minutes–1 hour, stirring occasionally, until the meat is tender. Taste and adjust the seasoning, then serve with steamed rice.

Cook's note
You could add some potato, if you like. Just peel and quarter a potato and add after the pork has been browned. Increase the red chilli powder to 1 tablespoon.

POULTRY AND GAME

SYRIAN-CHRISTIAN CHICKEN STEW

KOZHI CURRY

This stew is made for breakfast in Syrian-Christian households in Kerala and is traditionally served with *appams* – fermented rice batter pancakes cooked in a heavy iron wok. They have thin, crisp sides and a soft, fluffy centre and look beautiful, as they take the shape of the pan they are cooked in. Lovely as they are, they are also incredibly difficult to make unless you are very experienced and I have seen many a chef struggle with them. I've devised a special recipe for sweet and sour rice that uses the same flavours and therefore tastes just as good but takes away the element of uncertainty!

SERVES 4

3 tablespoons coconut oil or vegetable oil
5cm (2-inch) piece of cinnamon stick
6 cloves
4 green cardamom pods
4 garlic cloves, thinly sliced
5cm (2-inch) piece of fresh ginger, cut into thin strips
2 red onions, thinly sliced
8 green chillies, slit open lengthwise
10 fresh curry leaves
1 x 1.5kg (3^1/$_4$lb) free-range chicken, cut into 8 pieces
1 teaspoon salt
1 tablespoon black peppercorns, coarsely crushed
500ml (2 cups) coconut milk
3 tablespoons toddy (palm) vinegar (you could substitute sherry vinegar or white wine vinegar)
^{1}/$_2$ teaspoon garam masala

For the sweet and sour rice
2 tablespoons vegetable oil
2 star anise
4 green cardamom pods
2 bay leaves
1 onion, chopped
10 fresh curry leaves
1 teaspoon salt
1 teaspoon sugar
3 tablespoons white vinegar
220ml (scant 1 cup) water
5 tablespoons coconut milk
150g (^{3}/$_4$ cup) basmati rice, washed under cold running water, then soaked for 20 minutes

Heat the coconut or vegetable oil in a large saucepan and add the whole spices, followed by the garlic, ginger, onions, green chillies and curry leaves. Cook over a medium heat until the onions are soft. Add the chicken, salt and pepper and stir for a minute. Stir in the coconut milk, bring to the boil, then reduce the heat and simmer, covered, for about 45 minutes, until the chicken is cooked through.

Meanwhile, for the sweet and sour rice, heat the oil in a pan, add the star anise, cardamom and bay leaves and stir for 30 seconds or so, until they release their flavours into the oil. Add the onion, curry leaves, salt and sugar and cook gently until the onion is translucent. Pour in the vinegar, water and coconut milk, bring to the boil, then add the soaked rice. Mix well, stirring for 5 minutes or so, then lower the heat, cover the pan with a tight-fitting lid and cook for another 7–8 minutes. All the liquid should be absorbed by now. Remove the lid, stir the rice to open up the grains, then cover with the lid again and set aside, off the heat, for 10 minutes to cook in its own steam.

When the chicken is done, add the vinegar, sprinkle in the garam masala and mix well. Remove from the heat and serve with the sweet and sour rice.

Cook's note
You could cook this dish with boneless chicken meat if you prefer, though with chicken on the bone there is more flavour. If using boned chicken, choose just the thighs, cut in half, and cook them slowly until tender. Chicken breasts will cook much faster but tend to become dry and the dish will lack depth of flavour.

CHICKEN DRUMSTICKS COOKED IN A SEALED POT

DUM KA MURGH

This Hyderabadi speciality comes from the royal courts of Lucknow, where the techniques of smoking and cooking in a sealed pot over a low heat were perfected. The smokiness of the cloves and the richness of the nuts make this dish truly unique. It's one of my favourite recipes in the entire book.

It used to be quite common for marriages to take place between the royal families of the various courts in India, and each time the bride would bring an entourage of cooks, maids and other servants. This explains how some recipes made their way into different regions.

SERVES 4

3 tablespoons ghee or vegetable oil
2 bay leaves
3 green cardamom pods
1 teaspoon black peppercorns
2 x 2.5cm (1-inch) cinnamon sticks
3 blades of mace
$1/2$ teaspoon royal (black) cumin seeds
3 tablespoons Ginger-Garlic Paste (see page 202)
12 free-range chicken drumsticks, skinned
2 teaspoons salt
6 green chillies, slit lengthwise in half
500g (2 cups) plain yoghurt
$1/2$ teaspoon garam masala
2 tablespoons Crisp Fried Onions (see page 203)
a small bunch of mint leaves
a small pinch of saffron strands

For the pastes
120g ($1/2$ cup) broken cashew nuts, soaked in 750ml (3 cups) water for 30 minutes

2 teaspoons white poppy seeds, soaked in 120ml ($1/2$ cup) water for 30 minutes
3 onions, roughly chopped

To finish
4–6 cloves
1 teaspoon ghee
2 tablespoons single cream (optional)

First make the pastes. Place the cashew nuts and poppy seeds, along with their soaking water, in a blender or food processor and blitz to a smooth paste. Boil the onions in 500ml (2 cups) water until they are soft and most of the water has been absorbed, then blend to a smooth paste. Set the pastes aside.

Heat the ghee or oil in a large, heavy-based pan, add the bay leaves and whole spices and let them splutter. Now add the boiled onion paste and stir-fry for 8–10 minutes, until golden. Stir in the ginger-garlic paste and sauté for 3–4 minutes. Add the chicken drumsticks, salt and green chillies and stir-fry over a high heat for 6–8 minutes. Pour in the cashew nut and poppy seed paste and cook for another 5–6 minutes, stirring frequently to ensure that the paste does not stick to the bottom of the pan. Reduce the heat, pour in the yoghurt and bring to the boil, stirring continuously. Cover the pan with a tight-fitting lid and cook gently for 20 minutes. Stir in the garam masala and simmer for 8–10 minutes, until the ghee begins to separate from the

mixture. Now sprinkle in the fried onion, mint leaves and saffron.

To finish, place a small metal bowl containing 1–2 pieces of smouldering charcoal in the centre of the pan, put the cloves on the charcoal and drizzle with the teaspoon of ghee. Immediately cover the pan with a tight-fitting lid, making sure the emerging smoke does not escape.

Place the entire pot in an oven preheated to 180°C/350°F/Gas Mark 4 for 10 minutes. Remove from the oven, set aside for 5 minutes and then take the lid off. Remove the metal bowl. Check the seasoning and add the single cream to bring the sauce back together if the fat has separated out from it. Serve with pilau rice or a bread of your choice.

Cook's notes
If you don't want to try the charcoal method of smoking the dish, simply heat a tablespoon of ghee to smoking point in a small pan, add the cloves and let them splutter. Immediately tip the cloves over the curry and cover with the lid for 5 minutes or so, until the dish acquires a smoky flavour from the cloves.

The same dish garnished with halved or quartered soft-boiled eggs is known as Dum ka Murgh 'Asifi' in Hyderabad, probably paying respects to a Mr Asif who came up with this novel garnish!

JUNGLE CURRY OF COUNTRY CHICKEN WITH FRESH FENUGREEK

METHI WALA JUNGLEE MURGH

This is a very basic, rustic curry that could be made with any kind of chicken but works particularly well with free-roaming, older birds. Their meat is slightly tougher than that of young birds but there is so much more flavour.
In the past, when people cooked this outdoors over a wood fire with very basic implements, the spices would often be added whole and the vegetables roughly cut, hence the name jungle curry

SERVES 4

5 tablespoons vegetable or corn oil
5 cloves
2.5cm (1-inch) piece of cinnamon stick, broken in half
2 black cardamom pods
$1/2$ teaspoon black peppercorns
$1/4$ teaspoon fenugreek seeds
1 bay leaf
4 onions, finely chopped
1 tablespoon chopped garlic
1 x 1.2–1.5kg ($2^3/_4$–$3^1/_4$lb) free-range chicken, skinned and cut into 8 pieces
1 tablespoon Ginger Paste (see page 202)
2 teaspoons salt
$1^1/2$ teaspoons red chilli powder
1 teaspoon red chilli flakes
1 teaspoon ground cumin
1 teaspoon ground coriander
4 tomatoes, chopped
120g ($1/2$ cup) plain yoghurt
2 green chillies, chopped
500ml (2 cups) water
5 tablespoons fresh fenugreek leaves, blanched in boiling water for 1 minute, then drained and chopped
$1/4$ teaspoon garam masala
$1/2$ teaspoon dried fenugreek leaves, crumbled between your fingers
juice of $1/2$ lemon

Heat the oil in a large, heavy-based pan, add the whole spices and bay leaf and let them splutter. Once the spices change colour, add the onions and garlic and sauté until golden brown. Add the chicken pieces and stir-fry for 6–8 minutes over a high heat, until browned at the edges. Add the ginger paste, salt, chilli powder, chilli flakes, cumin and coriander and cook, stirring, over a high heat for 2–4 minutes. Add the tomatoes and cook for 8–10 minutes, stirring constantly to ensure that the spices do not stick to the bottom of the pan.

Once the oil starts to separate out from the masala round the edges of the pan, add the yoghurt and green chillies, reduce the heat and cook, stirring frequently, till the liquid comes to the boil again. Add the water, bring to the boil, then simmer over a low heat for 10 minutes or until the chicken is fully cooked. Stir in the blanched fenugreek leaves, followed by the garam masala, dried fenugreek and lemon juice. Serve with rice or chapattis.

Cook's note
To make this dish dairy free, you could replace the yoghurt with water.

BARBECUED HALF CHICKEN WITH TOMATO AND FENUGREEK SAUCE

This is the sort of dish where barbecue meets curry and has a lot of fun. The smokiness of barbecue cooking is reminiscent of the tandoor. Poussins are ideal here, cut in half lengthways and cooked on bamboo or metal skewers. I find this dish goes down particularly well at the end of a barbecue, when you want to settle down to something with a bit of sauce and a bit more substance.

SERVES 4

2 x 750–800g (1lb 10oz–1³/₄lb) poussins, skinned and cut lengthwise in half

For the marinade
2 tablespoons vegetable or corn oil
2 tablespoons red chilli powder
2 tablespoons Ginger-Garlic Paste (see page 202)
1 tablespoon ground cumin
1¹/₂ teaspoons ground coriander
250g (1 cup) plain yoghurt
1¹/₂ teaspoons salt
juice of 1 lemon

For the tomato and fenugreek sauce
12 very ripe tomatoes, roughly chopped
2 bay leaves
3 garlic cloves, peeled
2.5cm (1-inch) piece of fresh ginger, crushed
3 cloves
3 green cardamom pods
250ml (1 cup) water
2 teaspoons red chilli powder
60g (¹/₄ cup) unsalted butter
¹/₄ teaspoon garam masala
1 teaspoon dried fenugreek leaves, crushed between your fingertips

4 tablespoons single cream
1¹/₂ teaspoons salt
2 teaspoons sugar
1 tablespoon finely chopped coriander stalks

Wash the poussins, dry them on kitchen paper, then make incisions in the breast and legs at approximately 5cm (2-inch) intervals with the tip of a sharp knife. These incisions help the birds retain the flavours of the marinade and cook evenly.

Combine all the ingredients for the marinade in a large bowl, add the chicken pieces and mix well, Thread the chicken on to bamboo or metal skewers and place in the fridge for at least 30 minutes.

Meanwhile, make the sauce. Put the tomatoes, bay leaves, garlic, ginger, cloves, cardamom pods and water in a pan and bring to the boil. Simmer until the tomatoes have disintegrated, then remove the bay leaves and leave to cool. Purée the mixture in a blender and then pass it through a sieve to get rid of the tomato seeds and skin. Bring to the boil in a clean pan, add the red chilli powder and simmer for 5–8 minutes. Now add the butter and cook for 6–7 minutes over a low heat, stirring constantly so the butter does not split. Add the garam masala and crushed dried fenugreek and cook for 2–3 minutes. Pour in the cream and simmer until the sauce becomes thick and glossy.

Adjust the seasoning by adding the salt and sugar, then finish with the coriander stalks. Remove from the heat and keep warm.

Place the poussin skewers on a medium-hot barbecue and cook for 10–12 minutes on each side, until the birds are cooked through (or you could cook them under a hot grill). Pour the sauce over the barbecued poussins and serve with Naan Bread (see page 192).

Cook's note
If you have some of these cooked chickens left over, you could prepare the sauce without butter, pour it into a baking tray and place the chickens on top. Heat through in the oven at 180°C/350°F/Gas Mark 4 and serve dotted with knobs of butter and drizzled with cream.

CHARGRILLED MUSTARD CHICKEN WITH GREEN FENUGREEK SAUCE

This is a deconstructed *methi* chicken, where the legs and breasts are cooked separately and then put together on the plate to create layers of flavour and texture.

The recipe is actually easier than it looks, and I have found that by cooking the parts separately you create a delightful lightness of touch.

SERVES 4

4 chicken breasts, skin removed but wing bone attached
2 tablespoons vegetable or corn oil

For the marinade
1 tablespoon Ginger-Garlic Paste (see page 202)
1 teaspoon salt
$1/2$ teaspoon ground turmeric
1 teaspoon Dijon mustard
1 tablespoon plain yoghurt
1 tablespoon mustard oil
juice of $1/2$ lemon

For the green fenugreek sauce
3 tablespoons vegetable or corn oil
1 bay leaf
2 green cardamom pods
1 teaspoon cumin seeds
3 onions, finely chopped
2 green chillies, slit lengthwise in half
$1/2$ teaspoon ground turmeric
1 teaspoon red chilli powder
2 chicken thighs, boned and cut into 1cm ($1/2$-inch) dice
2 tomatoes, finely chopped
120g ($1/2$ cup) plain yoghurt
250ml (1 cup) chicken stock or water
1 teaspoon salt

5 tablespoons chopped fresh fenugreek leaves
$1/2$ teaspoon garam masala
1 teaspoon dried fenugreek leaves
$1/2$ teaspoon sugar

Mix together all the ingredients for the marinade, add the chicken breasts and coat well. Leave in the fridge for 20 minutes.

Meanwhile, make the sauce. Heat the oil in a heavy-based pan and add the bay leaf, cardamom and cumin seeds. When they crackle, add the onions and sauté over a moderate heat until golden. Add the green chillies, turmeric and chilli powder and sauté for 2 minutes. Now add the diced chicken thighs and cook for 8–10 minutes over a medium heat. Stir in the tomatoes and cook for 5–8 minutes, until the oil separates from the mixture. Add the yoghurt and cook, stirring continuously, for 3–4 minutes over a medium heat. Add the chicken stock or water and salt, cover the pan and simmer for 5–6 minutes. Stir in the fenugreek leaves, garam masala, dried fenugreek and sugar and simmer for 2 minutes. Remove from the heat and keep warm.

To cook the chicken, heat the oil in an ovenproof frying pan, add the chicken breasts and sear for 2 minutes on each side. Transfer the pan to an oven preheated to 200°C/400°F/ Gas Mark 6 and cook for 6–8 minutes, until the chicken is done. Serve the chicken on the sauce, with Masala Mash (see page 181) or steamed rice.

CHICKEN CAFREAL

This is the type of dish where anything goes. I've seen people cook it as a curry, grill it on a barbecue, serve it fried and even roast it in the oven. My favourite version is the roasted one, as it makes great gravy for dunking bread into. Carve the chicken at the table and don't bother with cutlery – go at it with your fingers and tear into it.

SERVES 4

1 x 1.2–1.5kg (2³/₄–3¹/₄lb) free-range chicken
juice of 1 lime
1 tablespoon chopped fresh coriander

For the spice paste
4 tablespoons vegetable or corn oil
5cm (2-inch) piece of cinnamon stick
6 cloves
4 green cardamom pods
4 star anise
4 garlic cloves, chopped
5cm (2-inch) piece of fresh ginger, chopped
5 green chillies, chopped
1¹/₂ teaspoons salt
1 teaspoon sugar
1 tablespoon ground coriander
1 teaspoon red chilli powder
1 teaspoon ground cumin
¹/₂ teaspoon ground turmeric
120g (1¹/₂ cups) coriander stalks, chopped
5 tablespoons grated fresh coconut
1 tablespoon Worcestershire sauce

To make the spice paste, put all the ingredients in a food processor and blitz to a paste. Rub the paste over the chicken, inside and out. Push some of the mixture between the skin and the flesh, taking care not to rip the skin. Set aside for 30 minutes.

Place the chicken in an oven preheated to 200°C/400°F/Gas Mark 6 and roast for about 40–45 minutes, until cooked through.Remove from the oven and leave to rest for 15–20 minutes. Reserve the juices.

To make the gravy, pour the reserved juices into a pan and simmer until slightly reduced. Adjust the seasoning, if necessary, and stir in the lime juice. Sprinkle the fresh coriander on top of the chicken, then serve with the gravy and hunks of baguette or similar bread.

Cook's note
If you want to reduce the cooking time, cut the chicken in half lengthwise, then marinate as above. Cook under a medium-hot grill for 15–18 minutes on each side. This not only reduces the cooking time but also gives a much crisper skin.

PARSEE-STYLE HOT AND SWEET CHICKEN CURRY WITH APRICOTS

SALLI MURGHI

This quintessential Parsee favourite is quite a big boy in terms of flavours and textures: dark, rich, sweet and spicy, crisp and soft all at the same time. It is one of the trademark dishes of the wealthy Zoroastrian community in Mumbai and one of the very few Indian curries to combine meat and fruit so successfully.

SERVES 4

4 tablespoons vegetable or corn oil
1 teaspoon cumin seeds
5cm (2-inch) piece of cinnamon stick
3 black cardamom pods
$1/2$ teaspoon cloves
3 onions, finely chopped
1 tablespoon Ginger Paste (see page 202)
1 tablespoon Garlic Paste (see page 202)
1 free-range chicken, cut into 8–10 pieces
2 teaspoons salt
3 tomatoes, puréed
4 tablespoons white vinegar
8 dried apricots, sliced
$1/2$ teaspoon sugar
1 tablespoon dark soy sauce (optional)
2 tablespoons chopped fresh coriander

For the spice mix
5 dried red chillies
5cm (2-inch) piece of cinnamon stick
1 teaspoon cumin seeds
2 black cardamom pods
5 cloves

For the potato straws
1 large potato (such as Desiree), peeled and cut into matchsticks
vegetable or corn oil for frying
$1/2$ teaspoon salt
$1/2$ teaspoon red chilli powder

For the spice mix, roast all the spices in a dry frying pan over a medium heat for a minute or so and then grind them to a fine powder in a spice grinder or coffee grinder. Set aside.

To make the potato straws, wash the potato matchsticks in cold water, then drain and pat dry on kitchen paper. Pour about 5cm (2 inches) of oil into a saucepan or a deep frying pan and heat to 180°C/350°F. Add the potato strips and fry for about 2 minutes, until crisp and golden. Remove and spread out on kitchen paper to drain. Sprinkle with the salt and chilli powder, mix well and set aside.

To make the chicken curry, heat the oil in a saucepan, add the whole spices and let them crackle. Add the onions, and cook, stirring, over a high heat until golden brown. Add the ginger and garlic pastes, followed by the chicken, and stir for 2–3 minutes, until the chicken begins to colour. Add the salt and puréed tomatoes and cook, stirring, for 6–8 minutes, until the liquid from the tomatoes has evaporated. Reduce the heat, cover the pan and cook gently for about 25 minutes, until the chicken is almost done. Add the ground spice mix, stir in the vinegar, apricots and sugar and cook for another 5 minutes. If the chicken doesn't have a rich glaze, add the soy sauce. Sprinkle in the coriander and remove from the heat. Serve the chicken curry garnished with the potato straws and accompanied by Brown Basmati Pilau (see page 180).

OLD DELHI-STYLE CHICKEN CURRY

MURGH MAKHANWALA

In the 1950s, the legendary Moti Mahal restaurant in Old Delhi created the dish that symbolises Indian food for millions of people all over the world. Also known as butter chicken, it's the dish to sell your soul for!

This happens to be the first curry ever to appear on the menu at The Cinnamon Club and, although it features in the original *Cinnamon Club Cookbook* (2003, Absolute Press) the recipe has evolved, so I'm including it here too. Besides, I can't imagine a curry book without butter chicken. Ideally it would be cooked in a tandoor oven to give a smoky flavour, but an ordinary oven or barbecue is a good enough alternative.

SERVES 4

1 x 1.2kg free-range chicken, skinned and cut into 4 pieces on the bone

For the marinade
2 tablespoons Ginger-Garlic Paste (see page 202)
1 tablespoon vegetable or corn oil
$1^1/_2$ teaspoons salt
juice of 1 lemon
2 teaspoons red chilli powder
120g ($^1/_2$ cup) Greek-style yoghurt
$^1/_4$ teaspoon garam masala

For the sauce
1.2kg ($2^3/_4$lb) tomatoes, cut in half
125ml ($^1/_2$ cup) water
5cm (2-inch) piece of fresh ginger, half crushed and half finely chopped
4 garlic cloves, peeled
4 green cardamom pods
2 cloves

1 bay leaf
1 tablespoon red chilli powder
80g ($^1/_3$ cup) butter, diced
2 green chillies, slit into quarters
5 tablespoons single cream
$1^1/_2$ teaspoons salt
2 teaspoons dried fenugreek leaves, crushed between your fingertips
$^1/_4$ teaspoon garam masala
$1^1/_2$ tablespoons sugar

Make small cuts all over the chicken pieces with a sharp knife to help the marinade penetrate. To marinate the chicken, mix it with the ginger-garlic paste, oil, salt, lemon juice and chilli powder and leave for 10 minutes. Then mix the yoghurt and garam masala together and apply to the chicken. Set aside for another 10 minutes, if you have time, or proceed to cook either on a barbecue on skewers or in an oven preheated to 220°C/425°F/Gas Mark 7 for 15–18 minutes. You may need to turn the pieces after 10 minutes or so to ensure they colour evenly on both sides. The chicken should be not quite cooked through. Strain off the juices through a fine sieve and set aside.

For the sauce, put the tomatoes in a pan with the water, crushed ginger, garlic, cardamom, cloves and bay leaf and bring to the boil. Simmer until the tomatoes have completely disintegrated. Now blend this tomato broth with a hand-held blender and pass it through a sieve to obtain a smooth purée. Return to

a clean pan, add the chilli powder and simmer for 12–15 minutes. It should slowly begin to thicken. When the sauce turns glossy, add the chicken pieces and the reserved roasting juices. Then add a cup of water and simmer for about 5 minutes.

Slowly whisk in the butter a couple of pieces at a time and simmer for 8–10 minutes, until the chicken is cooked through and the sauce is beginning to acquire a glaze. Add the chopped ginger, slit green chillies and cream and simmer for a minute or two longer, taking care that the sauce does not split. Stir in the salt, crushed fenugreek leaves and garam masala, then check the seasoning and add the sugar. Serve with Naan Bread (see page 192) or Pilau Rice (see page 180).

Cook's note
The beauty of this dish is that it is quite similar to French cooking, since the butter is added at the end to emulsify and enrich the tomato sauce. Not many people realise this, and cook it for too long after adding the butter, which can cause the sauce to separate and lose its richness. If this does happen, simply whisk in a couple of tablespoons of water and a tablespoon of cream to bring the emulsion back.

SPICE-ROASTED WHOLE CHICKEN

MURGH MUSSALAM

A grand celebration dish, this is one you will struggle to find on restaurant menus anywhere. It has long been considered the king of Indian dishes and this version makes it even more special by adding raw rice to the cavity of the chicken, which is cooked by the time the bird is ready.

SERVES 4

1 x 1.2–1.5kg (2³/₄–3¹/₄lb) free-range
  chicken
1 medium egg

For the marinade
2 tablespoons Ginger-Garlic Paste
  (see page 202)
1 tablespoon vegetable or corn oil
2 teaspoons salt
2 teaspoons red chilli powder
juice of 1 lemon
¹/₂ teaspoon garam masala
1 teaspoon dried fenugreek leaves
400g (1²/₃ cups) plain yoghurt
5 tablespoons Crisp Fried Onions
  (see page 203)
3 tablespoons Fried Cashew Paste
  (see page 202)
1 tablespoon chopped mint

For the filling
50g (¹/₄ cup) basmati rice, soaked in
  lukewarm water for 20 minutes
¹/₂ teaspoon royal (black) cumin seeds
1 tablespoon Crisp Fried Onions
  (see page 203)
¹/₂ teaspoon salt
a pinch of saffron strands

To finish
2 tablespoons single cream
1 tablespoon finely chopped
  coriander stalks
chat masala, for sprinkling

Mix together all the ingredients for the marinade and insert them carefully between the skin and the flesh of the chicken to spread the spices as much as possible, putting some inside the cavity as well. Set aside to marinate for 30 minutes. Reserve the excess marinade. Meanwhile, boil the egg for exactly 4 minutes, starting in cold water, then chill it in iced water. Peel and set aside.

Mix together all the ingredients for the filling and stir in just enough of the reserved marinade to bind the rice together. Now fill about a third of the chicken cavity with the spiced rice, place the egg in the centre of the cavity and then fill up with the remaining rice. Put the chicken in a roasting tin; you can use strips of foil to keep the legs crossed – this is important, as they cover the cavity, helping the rice to cook. Cover the tin with foil, place in the centre of an oven preheated to 200°C/400°F/Gas Mark 6 and roast for 40–45 minutes, basting half way through. Then remove the foil and cook for another 15–20 minutes. The skin should be golden and crisp; if you think it needs some more colour, place the bird under the grill for 2–3 minutes. The rice should be cooked by the time the chicken is ready. Remove from the oven and leave to rest for 20 minutes.

Strain off the juices into a small pan, add any remaining marinade and bring to the boil. Stir in the cream, correct the seasoning and finally stir in the fresh coriander. Sprinkle with chat masala and serve the whole bird at the table with the sauce on the side. Accompany with Pilau Rice (see page 180).

Cook's note
You could marinate the bird and stuff the cavity the night before and simply place it in the oven roughly an hour and a half before you need it. It's an ideal dish for preparing in advance and lets you get on with entertaining your guests while it's cooking.

TANJORE-STYLE CHICKEN CURRY

I consider this South Indian curry to be quite special, as its flavours are uncharacteristically clean and fresh compared to others from the south, which can be quite heavy on spicing. Tanjore, or Thanjavur as some call it, is certainly not known for its meat dishes but this one is a real winner.

SERVES 4

800g (1³/₄lb) chicken thighs, skinned, boned and cut in half

For the marinade
1 teaspoon Ginger Paste (see page 202)
1 teaspoon Garlic Paste (see page 202)
1¹/₂ teaspoons salt
¹/₂ teaspoon ground turmeric
4 green chillies, chopped
2 tablespoons vegetable or corn oil
juice of ¹/₂ lemon

For the green spice paste
100g (2 cups) fresh coriander, roughly chopped
25g (³/₄ cup) mint, roughly chopped
25g (2¹/₂ cups) fresh curry leaves
5 garlic cloves, roughly chopped
5cm (2-inch) piece of fresh ginger, roughly chopped
4 green chillies, roughly chopped

For the sauce
3 tablespoons vegetable or corn oil
30 fresh curry leaves
¹/₂ teaspoon mustard seeds
4 dried red chillies
1 onion, chopped
¹/₂ teaspoon ground turmeric
1 teaspoon red chilli powder
1 teaspoon ground coriander
2 tomatoes, chopped
100g (scant ¹/₂ cup) Boiled Cashew Paste (see page 202)
1 teaspoon salt
3 tablespoons single cream

Mix together all the ingredients for the marinade and rub them on to the chicken thighs. Set aside for 20 minutes.

To make the green spice paste, blend all the ingredients together in a food processor, adding a little water or oil if necessary.

Spread the chicken pieces out on a roasting tray and place in an oven preheated to 220°C/425°F/Gas Mark 7. Roast for 15 minutes, until about two-thirds cooked through, then remove from the oven and set aside.

For the sauce, heat the oil in a frying pan, add the curry leaves and fry over a high heat until crisp. Remove with a slotted spoon, drain on kitchen paper and set aside. Add the mustard seeds and red chillies to the oil in the pan. When they begin to crackle, add the onion and sauté until golden brown. Stir in the ground spices, followed by the tomatoes, and cook over a medium heat until the tomatoes have completely broken down and reduced by about half.

Add the cashew paste and salt and cook over a low heat, stirring constantly, until the oil begins to separate from the mixture. Add the chicken, along with any juices from the tray, and simmer for 5 minutes. Stir in the green spice paste and cook for another 5 minutes. Crush the fried curry leaves and add them to the pan. Stir in the cream, then remove from the heat and serve with steamed rice or Layered Parathas (see page 196).

DUCK CURRY WITH PEANUTS, SESAME AND TAMARIND

HYDERABADI BUTTAKH KA SALAN

The original version of the Hyderabadi favourite, *salan*, this is a beautiful dish with fragrant spices, complex flavours and a nutty richness.

SERVES 4

1 duck, cut into 10 pieces on the bone
$^1/_2$ teaspoon salt

For the sauce
2 tablespoons coriander seeds
1 tablespoon sesame seeds
1 teaspoon cumin seeds
100g (1 cup) desiccated coconut
4 tablespoons vegetable or corn oil
50g ($^1/_2$ cup) peanuts
4 dried red chillies
$^1/_2$ teaspoon mustard seeds
$^1/_2$ teaspoon black onion seeds
2 sprigs of fresh curry leaves
2 quantities of Boiled Onion Paste
  (see page 203)
1 teaspoon red chilli powder
$^1/_2$ teaspoon ground turmeric
1 litre (4 cups) water
1$^1/_2$ teaspoons salt
$^1/_2$ teaspoon sugar
2 tablespoons tamarind paste
25g ($^1/_2$ cup) fresh coriander, chopped

Place the duck pieces in a roasting tin, sprinkle with the salt and roast in an oven preheated to 200°C/400°F/Gas Mark 6 for 20–25 minutes.

Meanwhile, make the sauce. Mix together the coriander, sesame and cumin seeds and roast them in a dry frying pan over a moderate heat for a minute or so. Tip them out on to a plate and set aside. Roast the coconut in the same pan until golden and add to the seeds.
Heat a tablespoon of the oil in the pan, add the peanuts and fry until golden. Remove and combine with the seeds and coconut. Blend to a smooth paste in a food processor, adding as little water as possible.

Heat the remaining oil in a pan and add the red chillies and mustard seeds. When they crackle, add the onion seeds and curry leaves, followed by the onion paste, and cook for 8–10 minutes. Now add the nut and seed paste and stir over a low heat for a couple of minutes. Add the chilli powder and turmeric, followed by the roast duck pieces, and cook over a high heat for 2–3 minutes, stirring constantly. Pour in the water, reduce the heat and simmer for 30 minutes, until the duck is almost tender. Stir in the salt, sugar and tamarind paste and cook for 5–6 more minutes. Sprinkle in the coriander and serve with Pilau Rice (see page 180).

Cook's note
You could make the sauce separately and serve with seared duck breasts if you do not like bones.

HALF A DOZEN QUAILS IN SPICY CURRY

BATEYR MASALA

When the reign of the Nawabs was at its peak in Lucknow, *bawarchis*, or cooks, supplied a variety of foods to the *dyodhi* (literally, threshold of the door) of their patrons. The food came in trays covered with a dome-shaped frame draped in muslin, which was secured with a tape and sealed with *lac* (a kind of resin) in order to prevent anyone tampering with it. Come to think of it, in the 1750s this must have been quite an advanced system of home deliveries and take-outs!

A dish such as this one was for special occasions; or if a cook managed to lay his hands on some sand grouse or other exotic game, he would simply prepare the dish for a client that he knew would love it and take it along. Quite often he'd arrive unannounced and uninvited, and almost always his dish would be accepted and he would be rewarded for his efforts.

SERVES 6

6 large quails, weighing 250–300g (9–10oz) each, skinned
2 tablespoons Ginger Paste (see page 202)
2 tablespoons Garlic Paste (see page 202)
1 teaspoon ground turmeric
2½ teaspoons salt
100ml (scant ½ cup) vegetable oil or ghee
2.5cm (1-inch) piece of cinnamon stick
a blade of mace
2 black cardamom pods
1 tablespoon black peppercorns
½ teaspoon cloves
5 green cardamom pods
1½ x quantity of Fried Onion Paste (see page 203)

2 tablespoons ground coriander
450g (2 cups) plain yoghurt, whisked with ½ tablespoon roasted gram (chickpea) flour until smooth
1 teaspoon garam masala
2 tablespoons finely chopped fresh coriander
a few drops of rosewater
a pinch of saffron strands

Wash the quails inside and out under cold running water, drain on a wire rack and then pat dry on kitchen paper. Mix together 1 tablespoon of ginger paste, 1 tablespoon of garlic paste, ½ teaspoon of turmeric and 1 teaspoon of salt and rub them over the birds. Set aside for 10–15 minutes.

Choose a wide, shallow pan, preferably one that can hold all 6 quails comfortably and has a well-fitting lid. Heat the oil or ghee in it, then carefully place the quails in the hot oil, taking care not to crowd the pan. Cook over a high heat until evenly coloured on all sides, then remove the birds from the pan and set aside.

Reheat the oil, add the whole spices and stir for a minute to release their flavours. Add the onion paste and the remaining ginger and garlic pastes and cook over a medium heat for 5–6 minutes, stirring to prevent the pastes sticking to the bottom of the pan.

Add the coriander and the remaining turmeric and salt and cook for 6–7 minutes, until the fat begins to separate from the pastes.

Return the seared quails to the pan and mix carefully, taking care not to break the birds. Now pour over the whisked yoghurt, cover the pan, reduce the heat and simmer for 12–15 minutes, until the birds are cooked through. Remove the lid, stir the sauce to check the consistency and add a little water if necessary; the sauce should coat the birds lightly. Correct the seasoning if required. Stir in the garam masala and fresh coriander, then sprinkle in the rosewater and saffron. Put the lid back on and remove from the heat.

Serve with a pilau of your choice (see page 180).

Cook's note
This could also be made with other game birds, such as partridge, pheasant and grouse, so feel free and go game!

DRY-SPICE-CRUSTED GUINEA FOWL WITH YELLOW LENTIL SAUCE

This is a modern interpretation of a typical, everyday, middle-class Indian dish of *dal-roti* and *kukkad* – i.e. lentils, bread and country chicken.

SERVES 4

4 guinea fowl breasts, boned, skinned and each cut into 3–4 pieces
1 tablespoon vegetable or corn oil
4 wooden skewers, soaked in water for 30 minutes

For the marinade
1 tablespoon Ginger-Garlic Paste (see page 202)
1½ teaspoons salt
1 teaspoon red chilli flakes
1 teaspoon red chilli powder
½ teaspoon ground allspice
juice of 1 lemon
2 tablespoons plain yoghurt
1 tablespoon finely chopped coriander stalks

For the coarsely ground spice crust
2 teaspoons cracked black peppercorns
6 cloves, coarsely ground
2 teaspoons fennel seeds, coarsely ground

For the yellow lentil sauce
120g (²/₃ cup) yellow moong lentils (split yellow mung beans)
750ml (3 cups) water
1 teaspoon ground turmeric
1½ teaspoons salt
1 tablespoon ghee
1 dried red chilli
a pinch of asafoetida
1 teaspoon cumin seeds
2 garlic cloves, finely chopped
1 onion, finely chopped
1 tomato, finely chopped
1cm (½-inch) piece of fresh ginger, chopped
1 tablespoon chopped fresh coriander
juice of ½ lemon

For the marinade, mix together the ginger-garlic paste, salt, chilli flakes, chilli powder, allspice and lemon juice, then rub them over the guinea fowl breast pieces and set aside. In the meantime, mix half the coarsely ground spices with the yoghurt and coriander stalks. Apply this mixture to the breast pieces to complete the marinade, thread the guinea fowl onto the wooden skewers and set aside while you prepare the sauce.

To make the lentil sauce, rinse the lentils under cold running water, then place in a pan with the water, turmeric and salt. Bring to the boil, then reduce the heat and simmer for about 25 minutes, until the lentils have thoroughly disintegrated. Blend the mixture to a purée with a hand-held blender.

Heat the ghee in a heavy-based pan, add the whole dried chilli, asafoetida, and cumin seeds and let them crackle. Add the garlic, wait for it to turn golden brown, then add the onion. Sauté over a moderate heat until golden. Add the tomato and cook for 3 minutes, then pour in the puréed lentils. Stir in the ginger and coriander and bring to the boil. Adjust the seasoning and finish with the lemon juice.

To cook the guinea fowl, heat the oil in a large, ovenproof frying pan (big enough to accommodate the skewers) and sear the guinea fowl skewers for 2 minutes on each side. Sprinkle the rest of the coarsely ground spices over the guinea fowl, then transfer the pan to an oven preheated to 200°C/400°F/Gas Mark 6 and cook for 6–8 minutes. Serve on the lentil sauce, accompanied by bread or rice.

Cook's note
The guinea fowl could be replaced with chicken breasts or thighs and the skewers will cook every bit as well under a grill or on a barbecue.

MIXED GAME COOKED IN AN INDIAN WOK

KADHAI KA SHIKAR

Shikar is a Hindi term for hunted meat, and this kadhai-style preparation is a quick and easy way to enjoy whatever you may be able to lay your hands upon.

SERVES 4

1 grouse
1 partridge
1 quail
1 pheasant
3 tablespoons vegetable or corn oil
2 dried red chillies
1 teaspoon coriander seeds, crushed
$\frac{1}{2}$ teaspoon cumin seeds
$\frac{1}{2}$ teaspoon fennel seeds
2 bay leaves
2 onions, $1\frac{1}{2}$ finely chopped and $\frac{1}{2}$ cut
   into strips 1cm ($\frac{1}{2}$ inch) thick
4 garlic cloves, chopped
5cm (2-inch) piece of fresh ginger,
   chopped
2 green chillies, chopped
1 teaspoon red chilli powder
1 teaspoon ground coriander
$\frac{1}{2}$ teaspoon ground cumin
5 tomatoes, 4 puréed and 1 deseeded
   and cut into strips 1cm ($\frac{1}{2}$ inch) thick
$1\frac{1}{2}$ teaspoons salt
$\frac{1}{2}$ teaspoon sugar
1 tablespoon chopped fresh coriander
juice of 1 lime

For the spice mix
3 dried red chillies
1 tablespoon coriander seeds
2 teaspoons fennel seeds
1 teaspoon cumin seeds
1 teaspoon black peppercorns
2.5cm (1-inch) piece of cinnamon stick
$\frac{1}{2}$ teaspoon carom seeds

Skin the birds, then cut the breasts off the bone. You won't need the legs but you could keep them to use for another dish. Cut the breasts into strips about 1cm ($\frac{1}{2}$ inch) thick and set aside.

To make the spice mix, roast all the ingredients in a dry frying pan over a moderate heat for a couple of minutes and then pound them to a coarse powder using a mortar and pestle. Set aside.

Heat the oil in a wok or a large frying pan, add the whole spices and bay leaves and let them crackle. Add the finely chopped onions and sauté until golden. Add the garlic, ginger and green chillies and sauté for a minute. Stir in the chilli powder, ground coriander and cumin and cook for another minute. Add the puréed tomatoes and continue cooking until they are reduced by half. Add the meat and sauté over a high heat for 2 minutes to sear it quickly. Add the onion strips, reduce the heat, stir in the spice mix, salt and sugar and cook for another minute or so. Add the tomato strips and mix well. Sprinkle in the fresh coriander, squeeze in the lime juice and remove from the heat. Serve with Naan Bread (see page 192) and a light salad.

Cook's notes
The leg meat from the birds could be minced and prepared in the same spices as above to make a game *keema*, or game curry.

You could also use hare or venison in this dish.

ROAST GROUSE WITH BLACK LENTILS

This sort of dish makes me feel fortunate to be cooking in Britain. Although India has a rich tradition of game cooking, it has now disappeared, due to a complete ban on hunting for the last 60 years, and an entire generation of chefs has never cooked any kind of game whatsoever. This is my effort to reclaim and preserve the lost art of Indian game cooking.

The grouse need to be skinned, the breasts and legs removed, boned and trimmed, then the meat from the legs, plus any trimmings, minced. Your butcher should be able to do this for you, given a little notice.

SERVES 4

4 grouse, prepared as described above
1 tablespoon vegetable or corn oil
Black Lentils (see page 184), to serve

For the marinade
1 tablespoon vegetable or corn oil
$1\frac{1}{2}$ teaspoons salt
1 tablespoon Ginger-Garlic Paste
(see page 202)
1 teaspoon cumin seeds, roasted in a dry frying pan and then coarsely ground
8 cloves, roasted in a dry frying pan and then coarsely ground
1 teaspoon red chilli powder

For the mince
3 tablespoons vegetable or corn oil
1 bay leaf
2 dried red chillies
1 teaspoon coriander seeds, crushed
1 onion, finely chopped

1 tablespoon Ginger-Garlic Paste
(see page 202)
1 teaspoon red chilli powder
1 teaspoon ground coriander
$\frac{1}{2}$ teaspoon ground cumin
1 tomato, chopped
1 teaspoon salt
1 tablespoon chopped fresh coriander

Mix all the ingredients for the marinade together in a large bowl and gently fold the grouse breasts into it. Leave to marinate in the fridge for 30 minutes.

Meanwhile, for the mince, heat the oil in a pan and add the bay leaf and whole dried chillies, then the coriander seeds. Sauté for a minute or so, until they release their flavours. Add the onion and sauté until golden. Add the ginger-garlic paste and stir for a minute, then sprinkle in the chilli powder, coriander and cumin and stir for another minute. Now add the tomato and salt and cook for about 5 minutes, until the oil starts separating from the mixture. Stir in the minced leg meat and cook for 6–8 minutes over a medium heat, until the mince is done. Stir in the chopped fresh coriander.

To cook the grouse breasts, heat the oil in a frying pan, add the marinated grouse breasts and sear for 30 seconds on each side. Place the pan under a hot grill and cook for 1 minute. Remove from the heat, leave to rest

for 5 minutes, then serve with the mince and Black Lentils.

Cook's notes
If you don't like your game too strong, then it is advisable to bulk the minced leg meat up with about 100g (4oz) lean minced lamb or beef. Alternatively, you could boil the mince in salted water with a pinch of turmeric for 5–6 minutes to make it milder, then drain well.

The grouse goes equally well with Pumpkin Pickle (see page 190). The rich, sweet flavours of the pickle work very well with the earthy, musky flavour of grouse.

Take care not to over cook the breasts, as they dry up very quickly. Since it is a very lean meat, grouse is best cooked fast and served medium.

SPICED ROAST PARTRIDGE BREASTS WITH CURRIED PEARS

Mention this dish and it always reminds people of Christmas. It's quite appropriate, as both partridges and pears are at their best at that time of year. The combination of flavours is rather unusual but it felt right when I thought of it and it tastes fantastic.

SERVES 4

8 partridge breasts

For the first marinade
1 teaspoon salt
1 tablespoon Ginger Paste (see page 202)
1 tablespoon Garlic Paste (see page 202)

For the second marinade
2 teaspoons dried mango powder
2 tablespoons white vinegar
250g (1 cup) plain yoghurt
4 green chillies, finely chopped
1 teaspoon salt
2 tablespoons chopped coriander stalks
1 teaspoon garam masala
1 teaspoon sugar
3 tablespoons peanuts, roasted in a dry
　frying pan and then coarsely crushed

For the curried pears
2 tablespoons vegetable or corn oil
a pinch of asafoetida
1 teaspoon cumin seeds
1 teaspoon chopped fresh ginger
1 green chilli, chopped
2 pears, quartered and cored
150g ($2/3$ cup) plain yoghurt
1 teaspoon ground turmeric

Mix together all the ingredients for the first marinade, rub them over the partridge breasts and set aside for 10 minutes.

Mix all the ingredients for the second marinade with the partridge breasts, adding the peanuts last. Leave to marinate for 30 minutes or so.

Meanwhile, prepare the curried pears. Heat the oil in a large frying pan and fry the asafoetida, cumin seeds, ginger and green chilli for about 30 seconds over a high heat. Add the pears and toss for a minute. Add the yoghurt and turmeric and cook over a low heat for a minute or so, stirring constantly, until the pears are glazed and evenly coated with the sauce. Remove from the heat and keep warm.

Thread the partridge breasts on skewers and cook in an oven preheated to 200°C/400°F/ Gas Mark 6 for 6–8 minutes. Alternate the partridge with the pears on a platter and serve.

Cook's note
When you come to serving, if you feel the pears have soaked up all the sauce, just add half a cup of water and reheat to bring the sauce back. Serve immediately.

ROAST SADDLE OF RED DEER WITH PICKLING SAUCE

This is one of the dishes I am immensely proud of, and I believe it embodies what contemporary curry is all about. Game cooking is fast becoming a lost art in Indian cuisine and I feel passionately about preserving it. This recipe is a perfect example of combining old and new, East and West – the best of both worlds.

It first appeared on the menu at The Cinnamon Club in 2003, when it was probably the first dish to cross the £30 mark in an Indian restaurant anywhere in the world! Although it was well received, it was not perceived as a curry until 2006, when it won the UK Best Dishes Award for Best Curry. It goes to show how much curries have changed all around the world over the last few years.

SERVES 4

1kg (2¼lb) venison from the saddle, trimmed and cut into 4 steaks
1 tablespoon Rajasthani Spice Paste (see page 203)
1 tablespoon Greek-style yoghurt
3 tablespoons vegetable or corn oil

For the marinade
½ teaspoon salt
½ teaspoon red chilli powder
1 tablespoon vegetable or corn oil

For the pickling sauce
3 tablespoons oil, preferably mustard oil
1 teaspoon pickling spice mix (1 part mustard seeds, 1 part black onion seeds, 1 part cumin seeds, ½ part fenugreek seeds, 2 parts fennel seeds)
1 onion, finely chopped

½ teaspoon ground turmeric
200g (scant 1 cup) Boiled Cashew Paste (see page 202)
3 tablespoons Greek-style yoghurt
250ml (1 cup) lamb stock or water
4 green chillies, slit open lengthwise
1 teaspoon salt
1 tablespoon jaggery or molasses sugar
1 tablespoon chopped fresh coriander

Mix together all the ingredients for the marinade, rub them over the steaks and set aside for 30 minutes. Mix the Rajasthani spice paste and yoghurt together and set aside.

Meanwhile, prepare the sauce. Heat the oil in a heavy-based frying pan and add the pickling spice mix. When the seeds begin to crackle, add the onion and sauté until golden brown. Add the turmeric, followed by the cashew paste, and cook, stirring, over a medium heat for 5 minutes. Now whisk in the yoghurt and stir over a low heat for 5 minutes, taking care that it does not split. Add the stock or water, green chillies and salt and simmer for about 10 minutes, until the sauce thickens and gets a glaze. Stir in the jaggery or molasses and chopped coriander and mix well. Remove from the heat, cover and keep warm while you cook the steaks.

Heat the oil in a large, ovenproof frying pan, add the meat and sear over a medium heat for 5–6 minutes on each side, until browned all over. Transfer to an oven preheated to 200°C/400°F/Gas Mark 6 and roast for 6–8 minutes if you like your meat pink, longer if you like it cooked more. Remove the steaks from the oven and spread the Rajasthani spice paste and yoghurt mixture over the top. Place under a hot grill (or return to the oven) for 1–2 minutes, until the top is lightly browned.

Divide the sauce between 4 serving plates and place the steaks on top – you can slice them or serve them whole, as you prefer. Serve with Pilau Rice (see page 180) or Masala Mash (page 181) on the side.

Cook's note
If you want to prepare this for a dinner party or for more people, ask your butcher to bone and roll an entire saddle for you, then double the quantities of the other ingredients and simply marinate the saddle with all the spices, including the Rajasthani spice mix and yoghurt. Roast it in the oven at 200°C/400°F/Gas Mark 6 for about 15 minutes. Remove from the oven and let it rest for 15 minutes, then carve and serve. Nice and easy! Remember, since venison is so lean, it can dry out very quickly, so it is always best to cook it fairly rare and let it rest for long enough.

RABBIT COOKED IN A PIT

KHAD KHARGOSH

This typical hunter's dish makes a complete meal on its own. In the days of the princes and Rajput kings, it would have been cooked on hunting expeditions, the rabbit wrapped in leaves and baked in a pit dug in the ground. I have replaced the leaves with foil (and the pit with an oven!).

SERVES 4

4 rabbit legs
4 white tortillas or chapattis
2 tablespoons butter or ghee, melted

For the marinade
4 tablespoons Greek-style yoghurt
1 tablespoon Ginger Paste (see page 202)
1 tablespoon Garlic Paste (see page 202)
1 teaspoon red chilli flakes
2 tablespoons Crisp Fried Onions (see page 203)
1 teaspoon cloves, lightly roasted in a dry frying pan and then ground to a powder
1 teaspoon ground turmeric
2 teaspoons red chilli powder
2 tablespoons Fried Cashew Paste (see page 202)
5cm (2-inch) piece of fresh papaya or pineapple, blended to a paste in a mini-chopper
6 green chillies, finely chopped
6 tablespoons mustard oil
2 tablespoons chopped fresh coriander
1 1/2 teaspoons salt
1/2 teaspoon sugar

For the garlic chutney
20 dried red chillies
250ml (1 cup) malt vinegar
5 tablespoons vegetable or corn oil

1/2 teaspoon cumin seeds
2 heads of garlic, peeled and chopped
2 tablespoons tomato paste
1 teaspoon salt
2 teaspoons sugar
1 tablespoon chopped coriander roots
juice of 1/2 lime

First make the garlic chutney. Soak the dried chillies in the vinegar overnight, then blitz to a smooth paste in a food processor or blender. Heat the oil in a frying pan and add the cumin seeds, followed by the garlic and the chilli paste. Cook over a low heat for 20 minutes, stirring occasionally. Stir in the tomato paste, salt and sugar and continue to cook for about 10 minutes, until the mixture has reduced and thickened and the oil begins to separate from it. Sprinkle in the chopped coriander roots and squeeze in the lime juice. Mix well, remove from the heat and leave to cool. Store in the fridge.

To make the marinade, combine all the ingredients and mix well. Put the rabbit legs in a roasting tray, mix with the marinade and set aside for 15 minutes. Cover the tray tightly with foil, transfer it to an oven preheated to 180°C/350°F/Gas Mark 4 and braise for about an hour, until the meat is very tender. Remove the legs carefully and leave to cool.

Put the braising liquid in a pan and simmer until reduced to a thick, sauce-like consistency. Leave it to cool, then smear the legs with this sauce, coating them evenly on all sides.

Brush the tortillas or chapattis with the melted butter or ghee and wrap each one tightly around a rabbit leg. Trim off any excess, then wrap in foil, sealing it completely. Place in an oven preheated to 180°C/350°F/Gas Mark 4 and bake for 20–30 minutes, until the bread is crisp. Remove from the oven, carefully tear off the foil and serve with the garlic chutney.

ACCOMPANIMENTS

PILAU RICE

Broadly speaking, there are two ways of cooking rice: the boiling method and the absorption method. Plain boiled rice is the most commonly served in Indian households but pilaus, which are cooked by the absorption method, are much better as they retain more flavour and nutrients. They do rely on precise ratios and cooking times but the results are worth the effort.

SERVES 4–6

500g (2½ cups) basmati rice
3 tablespoons ghee
1 teaspoon cumin seeds
3 cloves
2 green cardamom pods
1 cinnamon stick
1 bay leaf
1 red onion, sliced
1 litre (4 cups) water
1 teaspoon salt
1 teaspoon chopped fresh mint
1 teaspoon chopped fresh coriander

Wash the rice under cold running water once or twice, then place in a bowl of cold water and leave to soak for 25 minutes (this reduces the cooking time and prevents the grains breaking during cooking).

Heat the ghee in a large, heavy-based casserole and add the whole spices and the bay leaf. When they crackle, add the sliced onion and sauté until golden brown. Now add the water and salt and bring to the boil. Drain the rice and add to the pan. Cover until it returns to the boil, then remove the lid and cook over a medium-high heat for about 6 minutes, stirring occasionally but keeping in mind that too much handling can break the rice grains.

When the water has nearly all been absorbed and you can see small holes on the surface of rice, sprinkle over the mint and coriander. Cover the casserole with a tight-fitting lid, reduce the heat to minimum and cook for 10 minutes (or cook in a very low oven for 10 minutes).

BROWN BASMATI PILAU

This is a healthier version of the traditional white rice pilau. Don't expect brown rice to be as light and fluffy but enjoy its interesting, nutty flavour.

SERVES 4-6

500g (2½ cups) brown basmati rice
3 tablespoons ghee or vegetable oil
1 teaspoon cumin seeds
4 cloves
1 bay leaf
1 small cinnamon stick
4 green cardamom pods
1 onion, thinly sliced
1.25 litres (5 cups) water
a few mint leaves, shredded
1 teaspoon salt

Wash the rice under cold running water once or twice, then leave it to soak in a bowl of cold water for 25 minutes.

Heat the ghee or oil in a heavy-based pan and add the cumin seeds, cloves, bay leaf, cinnamon and cardamom pods. When they crackle, add the sliced onion and sauté until light golden. Drain the rice, add to the pan and sauté for 2–3 minutes, taking care that the rice does not break. Now add the water, mint and salt and bring to the boil. Reduce the heat to low, cover and cook for about 20 minutes, until the rice is tender and the water has all been absorbed. Remove from the heat and stir the rice gently to mix. Cover the pan and leave to rest for 15 minutes or so.

Cook's note
Stirring the rice and turning it over gently after the water has been absorbed ensures that the grains are evenly cooked. By resting it for 15 minutes, you give the grains ample time to gain volume so that they don't stick to each other.

LEMON RICE

This is one of several types of dishes made from humble boiled rice in southern India and it makes you realise just how versatile rice can be. It adds colour, flavour and vibrancy to any dish it accompanies.

SERVES 4–6

400g (2 cups) basmati rice
3 tablespoons vegetable or corn oil
1 tablespoon mustard seeds
1 tablespoon chana dal (yellow split peas)
1 teaspoon urad dal (white urid lentils) – optional
20 fresh curry leaves
1 teaspoon ground turmeric
1½ teaspoons salt
juice of 3 lemons

Wash the rice under cold running water once or twice, then place in a bowl of cold water and leave to soak for 25 minutes. Drain well. Bring 1 litre (4 cups) of water to the boil in a saucepan and add the rice. Simmer, uncovered, for 8–10 minutes, until the grains are tender but not mushy. Drain through a sieve and set aside.

Heat the oil in a large pan, add the mustard seeds, chana dal and urid lentils, if using, and let them crackle. When they start to turn almost golden, add the curry leaves, then the turmeric, and stir for a minute (you may need to sprinkle in some water to prevent the turmeric burning). Add the cooked rice, salt and lemon juice and toss gently to mix well without breaking the rice grains.

MASALA MASH

Although masala mash is a term that's appeared on a lot of restaurant menus in the last few years, it was The Cinnamon Club that first started using it. Originally it was more of a spiced potato crush than a mash but it has evolved over the years to get closer to mash as we know it in the West.

SERVES 4

500g (1lb 2oz) floury potatoes such as Desiree, peeled and cut into chunks
4 tablespoons ghee
½ teaspoon cumin seeds
1 onion, finely chopped
¼ teaspoon ground turmeric
1cm (½-inch) piece of fresh ginger, finely chopped
2 green chillies, finely chopped
1 teaspoon salt
2 tablespoons single cream
1 tablespoon chopped fresh coriander

Cook the potatoes in boiling salted water until tender. Drain, mash thoroughly and set aside. Heat the ghee in a saucepan, add the cumin seeds, followed by the onion, and cook until the onion is tender. Add the turmeric, ginger and green chillies and stir for 30 seconds. Add the potatoes and salt and mix well over a low heat until the potatoes are heated thoroughly and coloured evenly by the turmeric. Add the cream, sprinkle in the coriander leaves and remove from the heat.

YELLOW LENTILS
TADKA DAL

This is India's everyday dal, compared to Black Lentils (see page 184), which is more for special occasions and tends to be cooked in restaurants rather than at home.

In most households the lentils would be served quite thin and watery, simply boiled and tempered with spices. The process of adding spices crackling in hot fat to cooked dal is commonly known as *tadka*, hence the name of this dish.

The flavours and spices vary from region to region. In Rajasthan they would simply use asafoetida, cumin and chilli, in the Punjab garlic, onion and tomatoes are added, while in southern India it's common to see lentils tempered with curry leaves, chillies and mustard seeds. The options and flavour combinations are endless.

SERVES 4–6

100g (½ cup) masoor dal (red lentils)
100g (½ cup) moong dal (split yellow mung beans)
1.2 litres (5 cups) water
½ teaspoon ground turmeric
2 teaspoons salt
2 tablespoons ghee
2 dried red chillies
a pinch of asafoetida
1 teaspoon cumin seeds
4 garlic cloves, finely chopped
1 onion, finely chopped
1 teaspoon red chilli powder
1 tomato, finely chopped
2.5cm (1-inch) piece of fresh ginger, chopped
2 green chillies, chopped
1 tablespoon chopped fresh coriander
juice of ½ lemon

Wash the red and yellow lentils under cold running water, then drain well. Put them in a pan with the water, turmeric and salt, bring to the boil, then reduce the heat and simmer for 30–40 minutes, until they are so thoroughly disintegrated that you cannot tell the different lentils apart. Remove from the heat and keep warm.

Heat the ghee in a heavy-based pan, add the whole red chillies, asafoetida, and cumin seeds and allow them to crackle. Add the garlic, wait for it to turn golden, then add the onion and sauté over a moderate heat until golden brown. Add the chilli powder and sauté for a minute or two. Add the tomato and cook for 5–6 minutes over a moderate heat. Throw in the ginger, green chillies and coriander, then pour the mixture over the lentils. Adjust the seasoning and finish with the lemon juice.

Cook's note
In some parts of the country, as many as five different types of lentils are used. You could include as many types as you can find; just make sure that most of them have had their husk removed, otherwise it changes the colour of the final dish.

Left to right
Yellow Lentils (this page);
Pumpkin Pickle (page 192);
Carrot and Peanut Salad (page 193).

BLACK LENTILS

Probably India's favourite lentil recipe, this northern speciality features in all Indian restaurants of any standing. Rich, creamy, earthy, musky and fragrant all at the same time, it is one of the most wonderful dishes you could ever come across. Bukhara in Delhi, which always features in the world's top 50 restaurants (the only restaurant in India to appear on this elite list), has had this dish on its menu since 1978 and sells over 60 litres of it every day!

SERVES 4–6

250g (1¼ cups) black urid lentils, soaked in lukewarm water overnight and then drained
2.5 litres (2½ quarts) water
4 tablespoons vegetable or corn oil
2 black cardamom pods
1 green cardamom pod
1 bay leaf
1 tablespoon chopped garlic
1½ tablespoons Ginger-Garlic Paste (see page 202)
1 tablespoon red chilli powder
1½ teaspoons salt
6 tablespoons thick tomato purée, or 6 large ripe tomatoes, puréed
100g (scant ½ cup) salted butter, diced
1 teaspoon dried fenugreek leaves, crushed between your fingertips
1 teaspoon garam masala
1 teaspoon sugar
4 tablespoons single cream

Place the drained lentils in a large pan with the water, bring to the boil and simmer for 1 hour or until they are thoroughly tender but not mushy.

Heat the oil in a large, heavy-based pan, add the cardamoms and bay leaf and let them crackle. Add the chopped garlic and stir until golden, then add the ginger-garlic paste and sauté for 3–4 minutes. Add the chilli powder, salt and tomato purée and cook for 5 minutes.

Pour the lentils and their cooking liquid into the pan and cook over a medium heat, stirring constantly, until they are mashed and thoroughly incorporated into the mixture. Add the butter a little at a time and keep stirring to prevent it separating. Stir in the fenugreek leaves, garam masala, sugar and cream and cook for 3–4 minutes, then remove from the heat. Serve as an accompaniment to another dish or with bread.

Cook's notes
Wash the lentils in 3–5 changes of water before you soak them; this will prevent them going murky during cooking.

Clockwise from top
Peanut Chutney (page 197);
Black Lentils (this page);
Kachumber (page 76).

CURRY LEAF AND TOMATO QUINOA

We've only had quinoa on the menu at The Cinnamon Club for a few weeks, so it's relatively new and we're quite excited about it. For people with a gluten intolerance, it's an absolute godsend. I've discovered that it cooks beautifully as a southern Indian *upma*, which is normally made with semolina, and it can even be substituted for rice in some recipes.

SERVES 4
(OR 2 AS A MAIN COURSE)

100g ($^2/_3$ cup) quinoa
2 tablespoons vegetable or corn oil
1 dried red chilli, broken into 3 pieces
1 teaspoon mustard seeds
20 fresh curry leaves
1 large onion, finely chopped
1 green chilli, finely chopped
1cm ($^1/_2$-inch) piece of fresh ginger, finely chopped
1 tomato, coarsely chopped
1$^1/_2$ teaspoons salt
$^1/_4$ teaspoon red chilli powder
$^1/_2$ teaspoon sugar
1 tablespoon finely chopped fresh coriander or basil
juice of $^1/_2$ lemon

Soak the quinoa in cold water for 15 minutes, then drain and rinse. Put it in a pan with 300ml (1$^1/_4$ cups) salted water, bring to the boil and simmer for about 15 minutes, until the grains are cooked but still retain some bite (quinoa develops a white ring round the circumference of each grain when it is about ready). Drain off any excess water.

While the quinoa is cooking, start preparing the tempering. Heat the oil in a heavy-based pan and add the red chilli and mustard seeds. Let them crackle and splutter for about 30 seconds, then add the curry leaves. As soon as they are crisp, add the onion and cook for 6–8 minutes, until starting to turn golden. Now add the green chilli and ginger and stir for a minute. Add the chopped tomato, salt and chilli powder and cook over a medium heat for 8–10 minutes, until most of the moisture from the tomato has evaporated and the mixture begins to come together.

Add the cooked quinoa and mix for a minute or two, until heated through. Finish with the sugar, coriander or basil and lemon juice. Mix thoroughly and serve hot.

ROASTED AUBERGINE, TOMATO AND POTATO CRUSH

This rustic, earthy accompaniment is quite versatile and goes with lots of things. In the summer I like to serve it with grilled fish dishes, while in the autumn it's good with stuffed breads. It also makes a great accompaniment to kedgeree.

SERVES 4

1 large aubergine
2 tomatoes
1 medium potato, boiled, peeled and mashed
2 green chillies, finely chopped
1cm ($^1/_2$-inch) piece of fresh ginger, finely chopped
1 tablespoon chopped fresh coriander
1 teaspoon salt
$^1/_2$ teaspoon sugar
juice of 1 lemon
1 tablespoon mustard oil

Prick the aubergine all over with a knife, then place in an oven preheated to 180°C/350°F/Gas Mark 4 and roast for 20–30 minutes, until soft. Roast the whole tomatoes in the oven for 15 minutes. Remove them both from the oven and leave until cool enough to handle, then peel. Place the aubergine and tomato flesh in a mixing bowl, add all the remaining ingredients and mash together well. Check the seasoning and serve warm.

Cook's note
You could make this with just aubergines or potatoes as well.

Opposite
Curry Leaf and Tomato Quinoa

GREEN PEA RELISH

I discovered this recipe only very recently, even though I grew up in the region that it comes from – the border of Bengal and Bihar, in eastern India – and I was totally taken aback by it. The sweetness of the peas is beautifully balanced by the kick from the garlic and mustard oil, and it is reminiscent of Japanese wasabi in both appearance and taste.

SERVES 4

300g (2 cups) fresh or frozen peas
2.5cm (1-inch) piece of fresh ginger, chopped
3 garlic cloves, chopped
3 green chillies, chopped
1/2 teaspoon salt
1/2 teaspoon sugar
1 1/2 tablespoons mustard oil
1/2 teaspoon mustard seeds
10 fresh curry leaves
juice of 1/2 lime

Place the peas, ginger, garlic, green chillies, salt, sugar, and 1 tablespoon of the mustard oil in a food processor and blitz to a smooth purée. Transfer to a bowl. Heat the remaining mustard oil in a small pan, add the mustard seeds and curry leaves and let them crackle. Remove from the heat and pour the mixture over the pea purée. Check the seasoning and finish with the lime juice.

ROASTED YELLOW LENTIL RELISH
SATTU KA MASALA

This rather spicy relish is extremely versatile and can be used as an accompaniment to a simple meal of steamed rice and vegetables or as a filling for bread. It's quite common in parts of eastern Uttar Pradesh, Rajasthan and Bihar and is particularly suitable for areas of dry, arid heat, as it helps water retention in the body.

SERVES 8–10

400g (14oz) roasted gram (chickpea) flour
about 5 tablespoons mustard oil, or the oil from hot mango pickle
2 red onions, finely chopped
4 garlic cloves, finely chopped
4 green chillies, finely chopped
2.5cm (1-inch) piece of fresh ginger, finely chopped
1/2 teaspoon carom seeds
1 1/2 teaspoons black onion seeds
3 teaspoons salt
1 tablespoon sugar
3 tablespoons chopped fresh coriander
4 tablespoons raisins
juice of 1 lemon

Mix together all the ingredients, adding more oil if necessary to help them hold together, and serve straight up. Alternatively you can use this relish to fill paratha dough (see page 196) and make stuffed parathas. They go really well with yoghurt and are great as a vegetarian main course.

Cook's note
The relish will keep in an airtight container in the fridge for up to a week.

Clockwise from top
Green Pea Relish (this page);
Pomegranate Raita (page 193);
Roasted Yellow Lentil Relish (this page).

TAPIOCA CHIPS

These make a great alternative to potato crisps, and add texture to any dish. They can be served with pretty much anything: to perk up a simple vegetarian or seafood dish or as a snack with a chutney or dip of your choice.

SERVES 4

vegetable or corn oil for deep-frying
1 medium-sized tapioca (cassava)
1 teaspoon salt
$\frac{1}{2}$ teaspoon red chilli powder
a pinch of sugar
a pinch of asafoetida

Heat the oil to 180°C/350°F in a deep-fat fryer or a deep saucepan. Peel the tapioca and slice it into thin rounds using a mandoline or a vegetable slicer. Quickly drop them one by one into the hot oil and stir with a slotted spoon to prevent them sticking together. Cook for 3–4 minutes, until golden and crisp. Remove and spread them out on kitchen paper to drain. Transfer to a mixing bowl while still warm, sprinkle with the seasonings and mix well.

PUMPKIN PICKLE

This is my mother's recipe for a sweet pumpkin pickle. I am a great fan of its rich, spicy flavours. It makes an excellent accompaniment to game dishes such as grouse or venison, it's fantastic with parathas and may even be used as a spread in sandwiches or to perk up wraps.

SERVES 4

4 tablespoons vegetable or corn oil
$\frac{1}{2}$ teaspoon fenugreek seeds
4 dried red chillies, broken into
  2–3 pieces each
700g (1lb 9oz) peeled pumpkin flesh, cut
  into 1cm ($\frac{1}{2}$-inch) dice
2 teaspoons salt
1 tablespoon red chilli powder
1 teaspoon ground turmeric
5 tablespoons sugar
2 teaspoons dried mango powder (or
  mango pickle from a jar)

Heat the oil in a pan, add the fenugreek seeds and dried red chillies and let them pop. Add the pumpkin and stir over a high heat for 3–4 minutes. Stir in the salt, chilli powder and turmeric, then reduce the heat, cover and cook until the pumpkin is soft and begins to break down. Stir in the sugar – the sweetness balances the heat and spice and also makes the pickle glossy. Finish with the dried mango powder or mango pickle.

POMEGRANATE RAITA

Raita is a common accompaniment to Indian meals. It helps take the heat off certain dishes, keeps the body cool in hot months and aids digestion.

SERVES 4

1 pomegranate
500g (2 cups) Greek-style yoghurt
1 spring onion, finely chopped
2.5cm (1-inch) piece of fresh ginger, finely chopped
2 green chillies, finely chopped
1 teaspoon cumin seeds, roasted in a dry frying pan and then ground
1 teaspoon salt
$^1/_2$ teaspoon sugar
1 tablespoon chopped fresh coriander

Cut the pomegranate in half and remove the seeds, gently tapping the halves with a rolling pin or the back of a heavy knife to loosen them. Reserve a few seeds for garnish. Combine the rest with all the other ingredients except the coriander leaves and mix well. Transfer the raita to 4 bowls, sprinkle the coriander and reserved pomegranate seeds on top and chill until ready to serve.

CARROT AND PEANUT SALAD

Known in India as a *koshimbir*, this is one of the few bona fide salads served there. The combination of carrots and peanuts is unique and works very well with the fresh flavours, especially when carrots are in season and taste sweet.

SERVES 4

50g ($^1/_2$ cup) roasted peanuts
3 large carrots, grated
1$^1/_2$ teaspoons salt
1 teaspoon sugar
juice of 1 lemon
1 tablespoon chopped fresh coriander

For tempering
1 tablespoon vegetable or corn oil
$^1/_2$ teaspoon mustard seeds
2 dried red chillies, broken into quarters
a sprig of fresh curry leaves

Crush the peanuts lightly in a pestle and mortar and mix with the rest of the ingredients.

To make the tempering, heat the oil in a small frying pan and add the mustard seeds and red chillies. When they begin to crackle and change colour, add the curry leaves, then pour the mixture over the salad. Mix well and serve.

Cook's notes
You can have all the ingredients prepared beforehand and assemble just before serving.

If you keep the salad for too long after mixing, the carrots and peanuts lose their crunch and it's not half as much fun.

NAAN BREAD

This humble bread from Delhi and Punjab is probably one of the tandoor's finest gifts to mankind. It is popular the world over and makes an excellent accompaniment to any curry. Try using it for sandwiches, rolls or even as a base for canapés, too.

MAKES 16

3 tablespoons caster sugar
2 eggs
400ml (1²/₃ cups) whole milk
750g (5 cups) plain white flour
1¹/₂ teaspoons baking powder
1 tablespoon salt
3 tablespoons vegetable oil

Mix the sugar, eggs and milk together until the sugar has dissolved. Sift the flour into a bowl and stir in the baking powder and salt. Add the milk mixture to the flour, stir to combine, then turn out on to a floured work surface and knead lightly to make a soft dough. Take care not to work the gluten too much, or the dough will become too stretchy. Cover with a damp cloth and leave to rest for 15 minutes.

Lightly knead the oil into the dough until thoroughly incorporated. Divide the dough into 16 pieces and roll each one out on a lightly floured surface into a circle about 10cm (4 inches) in diameter.

Traditionally naan bread is cooked in a charcoal-fired clay oven but instead you can preheat your oven, with some baking sheets in it, to 220°C/425°F/Gas Mark 7, then put the breads on the hot baking sheets and cook for 4–5 minutes. You might need to turn the bread over if the underneath starts to colour but the top is still pale.

Alternatively, crank up your grill to maximum power and keep it ready. Place a few large, heavy-based frying pans on the hob and, when they're good and hot, place two naan breads in each one and cook for a couple of minutes until they start to colour lightly underneath. Remove the pan from the hob and place directly under the grill for a minute or so, until the bread puffs up and colours a little. *Voilà*! Your naan bread is ready and you did not even need a tandoor oven.

Cook's note
You can get as creative as you like with toppings for naan: before baking, try sprinkling them with turmeric, crushed chilli, fresh coriander, garlic, grated cheese, pesto, sun-dried tomatoes, olives – quite simply anything you fancy!

SPRING ONION PARATHAS

These are one of my childhood favourites. Normally these triangular breads are quite plain but my mother used to spice them up with onions, ginger, chillies etc. They also include some ghee to act as a shortening, which makes them really crisp. Serve with a simple chutney or dip, or cut them into small pieces to serve as canapés.

MAKES 8

500g (3^1/$_3$ cups) plain white flour
2 tablespoons ghee
^{1}/$_2$ teaspoon carom seeds
^{1}/$_2$ teaspoon black onion seeds
3 green chillies, deseeded and finely chopped
1 red onion, finely chopped
2.5cm (1-inch) piece of fresh ginger, finely chopped
the green parts of 2 spring onions, finely chopped
1^1/$_2$ teaspoons salt
1 tablespoon chopped fresh coriander, preferably the stalks
180ml (^{3}/$_4$ cup) water
4 tablespoons vegetable or corn oil

Put 400g (2^2/$_3$ cups) of the flour into a bowl and rub in the ghee with your fingertips until it is evenly incorporated. Add all the remaining ingredients except the water and oil and mix well. Gradually add the water, little by little, and knead until it comes together into a very stiff dough. If necessary, sprinkle in an extra tablespoon or so of water. Cover with a damp cloth and leave to rest for 10 minutes.

Divide the dough into 8 pieces and shape each one into a smooth, round ball. Flatten each ball lightly with the palm of your hand. Roll out into a circle about 15cm (6 inches) in diameter,

dusting with some of the reserved flour. Brush some of the oil over the top and dust with more flour. Fold the dough in half to make a semi-circle, then brush with more oil and sprinkle with flour. Fold again to get a small triangle. Roll out carefully to make a larger triangle about 3mm (^{1}/$_8$-inch) thick.

Place the paratha on a hot tawa or in a heavy-based frying pan and cook over a medium heat for 2–3 minutes, until the dough begins to dry out and get specks of brown underneath. Turn and cook the other side. While the second side is cooking, brush the first side lightly with oil. Turn again and cook until the colour deepens underneath, brushing the top with oil again. Turn once more. You should see the layers open up as the bread cooks. Remove from the heat once both sides are golden and crisp. Wrap loosely in foil to keep warm while you cook the remaining breads in the same way.

Cook's note
Take care not to add too much water to the dough, as the vegetables give out moisture and will eventually soften the dough, making it difficult to achieve a crisp, layered texture.

LAYERED PARATHAS

This is probably the most frequently cooked bread in Indian homes. Naan is usually eaten only in hotels and restaurants. Made with wholemeal flour, parathas are very versatile and can be served for breakfast, lunch or dinner.

MAKES 8

400g (2$^2/_3$ cups) wholemeal flour
2 teaspoons salt
1 teaspoon carom seeds and/or $^1/_2$ teaspoon black onion seeds
200ml (scant 1 cup) water
2 tablespoons vegetable or corn oil
5 tablespoons ghee

Set aside about 4 tablespoons of the flour and put the rest in a bowl. Add the salt, carom and/or black onion seeds, water and oil and knead until everything comes together into a smooth, stiff dough. Cover with a damp cloth and leave to rest for 20 minutes. Divide the dough into 8 portions, shape them into balls and leave to rest for another 15 minutes.

Flatten each ball lightly with the palm of your hand. Sprinkle some of the reserved flour on it and roll out into a circle about 20cm (8 inches) in diameter. Brush the top with ghee and sprinkle with a little more flour. Fold the dough in half to make a semi-circle, then brush with more ghee and sprinkle with flour. Fold again to give a small layered triangle.

Roll out each triangle to make a large triangle, taking care not to roll the dough too thin or you will lose the layers in the bread – roughly 3mm ($^1/_8$ inch) thickness is fine.

Heat a heavy-based frying pan or a flat griddle over a high heat, place one of the triangles in it and cook for 2–3 minutes, until the dough begins to dry out and colours underneath. Turn and cook the other side, then reduce the heat to medium. Brush the top of the bread with ghee and turn it over again until it develops a deeper colour. Brush the top and turn again. You will notice that as the bread cooks it puffs up, opening out the layers. The application of ghee and flour between the layers facilitates this. Cook the remaining breads in the same way, wrapping them loosely in foil to keep warm while you wait for the rest to be done.

PEANUT CHUTNEY

This simple and delicious chutney goes well with South Indian curries and Oriental-style dishes.

SERVES 4

2 tablespoons vegetable or corn oil
180g (1¾ cups) skinned peanuts
½ teaspoon red chilli powder
3 garlic cloves, roughly chopped
1cm (½-inch) piece of fresh ginger, roughly chopped
2 red chillies, roughly chopped
1 teaspoon salt
1 teaspoon sugar
4 tablespoons coconut milk
juice of 1 lemon

Heat the oil in a frying pan, add the peanuts and fry until golden. Remove from the heat and leave to cool.

Put all the ingredients in a food processor and blend to a paste. Check the seasoning and serve at room temperature.

Cook's note
You could replace the peanuts with cashew nuts if you wished. You could also thin the chutney with additional coconut milk and a little water to make a peanut sauce.

GREEN COCONUT CHUTNEY

Serve this simple yet versatile chutney to accompany any southern Indian dish. Mint is my little addition; you could also use tomatoes and red chillies for a red chutney, or even green mangoes for a fresh, sharp chutney.

SERVES 4

1 coconut, grated
50g (1 cup) fresh coriander leaves
20g (½ cup) fresh mint leaves
4 green chillies, chopped
2 tablespoons roasted chana dal
1 teaspoon salt

For tempering
1 tablespoon vegetable or corn oil
10 fresh curry leaves
¼ teaspoon mustard seeds

Put the coconut, coriander, mint, chillies, chana dal and salt in a blender or food processor and blend to a soft, spoonable consistency. To temper the chutney, heat the oil to smoking point in a small pan and add the curry leaves and mustard seeds. As soon as they start to crackle, add the chutney and remove the pan from the heat.

LASSI

This popular Punjabi drink is often served as an aperitif in Indian restaurants and comes in various guises. It can be served sweet or salted (see Chaas, below), thick (to be enjoyed as a nourishing drink) or thin (as a summer cooler). You can flavour lassis with rosewater, ripe mango or dried fruits. You will find it served in tall, stainless steel glasses and it is almost a meal on its own. In India, it is common to serve lassi with curries, as you would wine with food in the West; there is no tradition of drinking alcohol with a meal there.

MAKES 1 LITRE (4 CUPS)

700g (2¾ cups) plain yoghurt
300ml (1¼ cups) iced water
4 tablespoons sugar
a few drops of rosewater

Blend everything together in a blender or food processor and serve in tall glasses.

CHAAS

The Rajasthani version of the lassi. Chaas is served really thin, salted and spiced with cumin, ginger and chillies. It's known to be a digestive aid, as well as an effective thirst quencher.

MAKES 1 LITRE (4 CUPS)

500g (2 cups) plain yoghurt
500ml (2 cups) iced water
2 green chillies, deseeded, finely chopped
1cm (½-inch) piece of fresh ginger, finely chopped
½ tablespoon finely chopped fresh coriander
2 teaspoons salt
1 teaspoon cumin seeds, roasted in a dry frying pan and then crushed
1 tablespoon vegetable oil
¼ teaspoon asafoetida

Whisk together the yoghurt, water, chillies, ginger, coriander, salt and cumin seeds. In a small pan, heat the oil and add the asafoetida. Stir for 20 seconds or so, until the flavours are released, then pour it over the yoghurt and mix thoroughly. Serve chilled.

CUMIN COOLER
JAL JEERA

A wonderfully refreshing drink, especially on a hot day.

MAKES 1 LITRE (4 CUPS)

50g (2½ cups) mint leaves
1 litre (4 cups) water
1 tablespoon cumin seeds, roasted in a dry frying pan and then crushed
1½ tablespoons fennel seeds, roasted in a dry frying pan and then crushed
juice of 4 lemons
1 teaspoon ground black pepper
2 tablespoons salt
6 tablespoons sugar

Add the mint leaves to the water and chill for 30 minutes. Remove the mint, reserve 15–20 small leaves for garnish and muddle the rest to a fine paste using a mortar and pestle. Return them to the water, then strain through a sieve to remove any coarse bits. Add the rest of the ingredients to the water and stir well. Check the seasoning; the flavours should be quite intense from the mint, cumin, salt and sugar.

Take 6 chilled glasses and fill them about a third full with crushed ice. Pour over the cumin drink, garnish with the reserved mint leaves and serve immediately.

Left to right
Cumin Cooler; Lassi.

BASICS

GINGER PASTE

MAKES ABOUT 6 TABLESPOONS

175g (6oz) fresh ginger, peeled
5 tablespoons water

Chop up the ginger and process it to a paste with the water in a food processor or blender. The paste will keep for 1 week in the fridge.

GARLIC PASTE

MAKES 6–8 TABLESPOONS

175g (6oz) garlic, peeled
5 tablespoons water

Chop up the garlic and process it to a paste with the water in a food processor or blender. The paste will keep for 1 week in the fridge, but if you substitute oil for water it should keep for 2 weeks.

GINGER-GARLIC PASTE

MAKES ABOUT 10 TABLESPOONS

100g (3$^1/_2$oz) fresh ginger, peeled
100g (3$^1/_2$oz) garlic, peeled
175ml ($^3/_4$ cup) water

Chop up the ginger and garlic and process them to a paste with the water in a food processor or blender. The paste will keep for 1 week in the fridge.

FRIED CASHEW PASTE

MAKES ABOUT 300G (11OZ)

200g (2 cups) cashew nuts
2 tablespoons vegetable or corn oil
200ml (scant 1 cup) water

Fry the cashew nuts in the oil until golden, then remove from the pan with a slotted spoon. Soak them in the water for 20 minutes, then drain. Blend to a smooth paste in a food processor or blender with 5 tablespoons of water. The paste will keep for 4 days in the fridge.

BOILED CASHEW PASTE

MAKES ABOUT 400G (14OZ)

200g (2 cups) cashew nuts
1 blade of mace
1 green cardamom pod
300ml (1$^1/_4$ cups) water

Soak the cashew nuts in enough water to cover for 10 minutes, then drain. Put them in a pan with the mace, cardamom and water, bring to the boil and simmer for 25 minutes. Remove from the heat and leave to cool. Blend to a smooth paste in a food processor or blender with 100ml (scant $^1/_2$ cup) water. The paste will keep for 4 days in the fridge.

CRISP FRIED ONIONS

MAKES ABOUT 110G (4OZ)

600g (1lb 5oz) onions, sliced
at least 600ml (2½ cups) vegetable or corn oil for
  deep-frying

Deep-fry the onions in medium-hot oil until golden
brown, then remove and drain on kitchen paper. Store in
an airtight container for up to a week.

FRIED ONION PASTE

MAKES ABOUT 150G (5OZ)

Prepare Crisp Fried Onions as above, then put them in
a food processor or blender with 200ml (scant 1 cup)
water and process until smooth. The paste will keep for
1 week in the fridge.

BOILED ONION PASTE

MAKES ABOUT 300G (11OZ)

1 large onion, cut into 2.5cm (1-inch) dice
250ml (1 cup) water

Put the onion and water in a small pan and simmer for
15–20 minutes, until the onion is soft. Purée in a food
processor or blender until smooth. The paste will keep
for 3 days in the fridge.

RAJASTHANI SPICE PASTE

This can be used with game, chicken or any other kind
of meat, and even some types of fish – red snapper is
particularly good.

2 tablespoons mustard oil or sunflower oil
2 tablespoons ghee
1 large onion, sliced
6 garlic cloves, chopped
20 cloves
10 green cardamom pods
1 tablespoon coriander seeds
1 teaspoon black peppercorns
1 tablespoon fennel seeds
150g (3 cups) fresh coriander leaves, chopped
1 teaspoon salt
150g (⅔ cup) plain yoghurt

Heat the mustard or sunflower oil in a heavy-based
frying pan until smoking, then add the ghee. Add the
sliced onion and cook until softened but not coloured.
Add the garlic and cook for a few minutes, until it starts
to brown. Add the cloves, cardamom, coriander seeds,
peppercorns and fennel seeds in that order and stir
quickly over a high heat for a couple of minutes, taking
care that the spices do not burn. Stir in the coriander
and salt, then remove from the heat and leave to cool.
Transfer the mixture to a food processor or blender,
add the yoghurt and blend to a paste.

MACE AND CARDAMOM POWDER

MAKES ABOUT 10 TEASPOONS

$^1/_4$ nutmeg
40g (1$^1/_2$oz) blades of mace
50g (1$^3/_4$oz) green cardamom pods

Grate the nutmeg or pound it with a mortar and pestle to break it up. Dry all the spices in a microwave for 30 seconds, then grind them to a fine powder, using a spice grinder. Store in an airtight container and use within a week.

GARAM MASALA

There are many versions of garam masala; this is a good basic one. It is generally added to dishes towards the end of cooking to impart flavour, not to add heat as its name might suggest (*garam* means hot and *masala* means mix).

I would always recommend making your own garam masala if possible. Commercial blends use a larger proportion of the cheaper spices and less of the more expensive aromatic ones, such as cardamom and cinnamon.

50g (1$^3/_4$oz) coriander seeds
50g (1$^3/_4$oz) cumin seeds
20 green cardamom pods
10 cinnamon sticks, about 2.5cm (1 inch) long
2 tablespoons cloves
10 blades of mace
10 black cardamom pods
$^1/_2$ nutmeg
1 tablespoon black peppercorns
4 bay leaves

Put all the ingredients on a baking tray and place in a low oven (about 110°C/225°F/Gas Mark $^1/_4$) for 3–5 minutes; this intensifies the flavours. You could even dry the spices in a microwave for 20 seconds or so.

Grind everything to a fine powder in a spice grinder, then sieve the mixture to remove any husks or large particles. Store in an airtight container and use within 2 weeks.

ROASTING (AND CRUSHING) SEEDS

Put the seeds in a moderately hot frying pan or under the grill and roast for a minute or two, until they are just dried but not coloured. Remove from the heat and allow to cool to room temperature, then pound in a mortar and pestle until the seeds are crushed but still coarse enough to be identified separately. If you want to grind the seeds to a powder, the best way to do this is in a spice grinder.

GLOSSARY

ASAFOETIDA

This essential Indian flavouring has a very unpleasant smell and taste, so is never used alone, but when added to a dish it somehow rounds off the flavours. It is sold as a powder or granules and will keep well for up to a year. In addition to its culinary uses, asafoetida is reputed to be a cure for flatulence and helpful for respiratory problems such as asthma.

CAROM SEEDS (AJOWAN)

Closely related to cumin, which it resembles in appearance and fragrance, carom has a hot, bitter taste. When it is cooked with other ingredients, however, the flavour mellows. It is particularly good in fish and seafood dishes and with root vegetables.

CHANA DAL

This is essentially split yellow peas from which the husk has been removed. A very versatile ingredient, it is used in many different forms in various parts of the country and is cooked as a pulse on its own in Bengal and eastern India. Chana dal is also used to make gram flour (see page 206).

CHAT MASALA

This spice mix typically consists of dried mango powder, cumin, black salt, dried ginger, coriander seeds, black pepper and sugar. It is used as a seasoning to perk up street snacks (known as chaats in Hindi) and various tandoori kebabs. On its own, it is rather an acquired taste, although it can be added to all sorts of everyday items. Ready-prepared chat masala is available in Indian and Asian grocery shops.

CURRY LEAVES

Curry leaves can be found pretty much all over India, right from the Himalayan foothills in the north to the southern coast and Sri Lanka. Curry leaves are to southern Indian cuisine what coriander leaves are to the north. Although readily available dried in the UK, they are much better bought fresh from Indian stores, where they may be labelled meetha neem or *kari* (sometime kadhi) patta. They will keep in an airtight bag in the fridge for at least a week and can also be frozen. Although dried curry leaves have little flavour, fresh leaves, when bruised, are very aromatic. They give off an intense, spicy aroma with a citrus note and have a warm, lemony, slightly bitter taste.

DRIED MANGO POWDER

Also known as amchoor, this is made by drying unripe green mangoes and grinding them to a tart powder. Pale beige to brownish in colour, with a sour, tangy, fruit flavour, it is used to add acidity to dishes, especially in northern India. It is popular in vegetable stir-fries, soups, curries, and for tenderising meat and poultry.

DRIED POMEGRANATE SEEDS (ANARDANA)

Sun-dried pomegranate seeds are used in both Indian and Iranian cooking and impart a sweet-sour flavour to various curries. Pomegranate has recently acquired the status of 'superfood' and the seeds are thought to have beneficial health properties. On another note, this is one of the very few ingredients that are used in Indian cooking to add texture.

FENUGREEK

The fresh leaves of this aromatic plant are eaten as a vegetable; dried fenugreek leaves (kasoori methi) are used to flavour all sorts of Indian savouries and curries. The best-quality kasoori methi comes from Qasoor in Pakistan.

Fenugreek seeds are used as a spice. Ancient herbalists prescribed them to aid digestion, a remedy that continues to be used today.

GHEE

This is clarified butter, the pure butterfat, clear and golden in colour. Traditionally in India, ghee is made from buffalo milk, which is higher in fat than cow's milk. The process involves souring the milk to make yoghurt and then churning this to yield butter. Unsalted butter made from cow's milk can also be clarified to make ghee.

GRAM FLOUR/ROASTED GRAM FLOUR

Also known as besan, gram (chickpea) flour is obtained by husking split yellow peas (chana dal) and then grinding them into a powder. It is a very versatile flour, commonly used in fritter batters, dumplings and to make bread. Gram flour can be stored in an airtight jar for up to 6 months.

Roasted gram flour (daria dal) is another form in which chickpeas are available in India. The split peas are roasted first and then ground to make flour. Roasting takes away the raw taste of the flour and increases its ability to retain water; it is often used as a thickening agent.

JAGGERY

Jaggery is a term used loosely to refer to unrefined sugar from both sugar cane and palm. If you cannot find it, dark molasses sugar can be substituted. Jaggery is considered by some to be particularly wholesome since, unlike refined sugar, it retains some minerals and there are no chemicals involved in its processing; it also enters the bloodstream more slowly than refined sugar. Indian Ayurvedic medicine considers jaggery to be beneficial in treating various lung and throat ailments.

KEWRA (SCREWPINE ESSENCE) AND ROSEWATER

Essences have been an important part of Indian cookery since antiquity. During the time of the Mughal emperors, rare flowers were grown in the royal greenhouses to make attars, or fragrant essential oils, and some of these turned up in the kitchen. Floral essences such as rosewater and kewra are the most popular today, used to flavour biryanis, pulaos, kebabs, desserts and treats.

Kewra is available from most Asian stores, though rosewater can be substituted if necessary. It's never a problem to omit it from a recipe if you find it hard to get.

KOKUM BERRIES

Kokum is a dried fruit from the mangosteen family, sold either whole, as berries, or deseeded. Tart and astringent, it is often used in South Indian and Goan cooking instead of tamarind, vinegar or lemon juice to impart colour and sourness.

MUSTARD OIL

As the name suggests, this oil is extracted from mustard seeds. It is pungent in taste and smell and deep gold in colour. Mustard oil is greatly favoured in Bengal and eastern India, and certain Rajasthani dishes get their flavour from it. When used, the oil is usually heated almost to smoking point first, then cooled down and reheated again, to tone down its aroma.

PANEER

An Indian version of cottage cheese, paneer is made by curdling milk with lemon juice to separate the curds from the whey. The solids are then collected in a piece of muslin, tied and pressed under a heavy weight for a few hours to set. On its own, paneer tastes quite bland but it is widely used in vegetarian dishes.

TAMARIND PASTE

The pulp from tamarind is sold in most Asian shops in the UK and needs to be soaked in water and then strained before use. Ready-prepared tamarind paste is available too, in supermarkets and Asian shops. It can be used to flavour sauces, impart acidity to dishes and even as a thickening agent.

Tamarind comes from a tropical tree native to Africa, but it was introduced into India so long ago that it has often been reported as indigenous there. It was from India that it reached the Persians and Arabs, who called it tamar hindi, or Indian date. In Thailand, there is a carefully cultivated sweet variety with little or no tartness, grown specifically to be eaten as a fresh fruit.

INDEX

A NOTE FOR AMERICAN READERS

In the recipes, American measures are given in brackets after the metric measures. Below are the American terms for some of the ingredients and equipment used in this book.

Aubergine eggplant
Beetroot beets
Bicarbonate of soda baking soda
Caster sugar superfine sugar
Coriander cilantro (when referring to the green, leafy herb rather than the seeds)
Frying pan skillet
Greek yoghurt thick plain yoghurt
Grill broiler
Grilled broiled
Hard-boiled egg hard-cooked egg
Kitchen paper paper towels
Minced meat ground meat
Muslin cheesecloth
Pepper, red or green bell pepper, red or green
Plain flour all-purpose flour
Prawns shrimp
Sieve strainer
Single cream light cream
Spring onion scallion
Tomato purée tomato paste
Wholemeal flour whole wheat flour

ACKNOWLEDGEMENTS

Firstly to my mother, who has been cooking curry for over 40 years now. At an average of five dishes a day, six days a week, she has cooked close to 50,000 curries! Roughly a quarter of a million meals!

Jon Croft, for coming up with the idea of a curry book. It made me realise how little I knew of the subject and how much I'd forgotten.

Abdul Yaseen, Hari Nagaraj, Rakesh Nair, James Mossman, Imamuddin Khan and the rest of the team at The Cinnamon Club, who were all so excited and have contributed in their own ways. I could never have imagined a book on curry would inspire so much enthusiasm! They are the best team one could ask for.

Cristian Barnett, for making it fun to photograph curry. It was the most daunting aspect of the book and he made it seem effortless. Cristian, you have made curry look good!

Matt Inwood at Absolute Press, for his art direction; he gives the book its edge.

Jane Middleton, for her patience, being so fabulous yet firm, and for making sure the recipes work. I don't know a better person to edit this book and I can't possibly thank her enough.

Finally Archana, my wife, for putting things in perspective. It was so easy to get carried away one way or the other with a book like this.